Rethinking Return on Investment:
The Challenge of Accountable Meaningful Use

Pam Arlotto, MBA, FHIMSS, Editor
with
Susan Irby, BIE, MSHS, Associate Editor

HIMSS Mission

To lead healthcare transformation through the effective use of health information technology.

About the Editor

Pam Arlotto, MBA, FHIMSS, is CEO and President of Maestro Strategies. She is a nationally known speaker and thought leader in clinical transformation and high-value healthcare. Ms. Arlotto is a former Chair of the HIMSS Board of Directors and in 2011 was honored by HIMSS as one of its top 50 leaders for the Society's 50th anniversary. Ms. Arlotto authored and led the development of the award-winning series *Return on Investment: Maximizing the Value of Healthcare Information Technology* and *Beyond Return on Investment: Expanding the Value of Healthcare Information Technology*. She coined the phrase "Accountable Meaningful Use" as the value optimization strategy for healthcare.

About the Associate Editor

Susan Irby, BIE, MSHS, has over 25 years of healthcare experience across a broad range of healthcare functions, both strategic and operational. Her background is based in strategic planning work, including core business development, corporate master planning, physician manpower planning, integrated network development, managed care design and resource allocation modeling. This is supplemented by work in the areas of value realization with a focus on return-on-investment strategy and planning. Ms. Irby co-authored *Beyond Return on Investment: Expanding the Value of Healthcare Information Technology* and led the development of Maestro Strategies' *ROI Toolkit.*©

About the Contributors

Lori Bishop, MBA, is a finance and operations executive with over 20 years of leadership experience in the healthcare, information technology, logistics and hospitality industries. Her expertise is grounded in analytic sciences and practical application of strategy, financial analysis, technology and operational design. Ms. Bishop has over 10 years of healthcare industry experience specifically focused on decision science and operational effectiveness.

Marla H. Crockett, BSN, MBA, has been working in the areas of strategic planning, transformation services, leadership development, clinical information systems, operational analysis and process redesign for more than 25 years. A former partner in the Healthcare Consulting Practice of Deloitte Consulting, Ms. Crockett has also served as Chief Technology Officer for a healthcare IT firm and Associate Executive Director, Patient Services, for Humana. Crockett was a contributor to *Beyond Return on Investment: Expanding the Value of Healthcare Information Technology.*

Bryant Hoyal, BSIE, PMP, is a healthcare technology leader with 15 years experience in the industry. She has successfully led clients through system implementation, process redesign, vendor selection, revenue cycle optimization, quality improvement reporting, resource utilization analysis, clinical pathways development, managed care contract negotiations and ROI analysis.

Kevin Martin, BSIE, MBA, utilizes his extensive Process Improvement experience to help hospitals better utilize existing facilities and resources more efficiently and effectively. He has a broad range of project leadership in healthcare operations including CPOE, Meaningful Use, Surgery, Emergency Department, Pharmacy, Lab and Materials Management. Mr. Martin has over 15 years experience and is a Lean Six Sigma Black Belt.

Vicki Miller, MBA, has over 25 years of healthcare experience across the provider, consulting and vendor areas including operations, finance, revenue cycle, marketing, strategy and business development. A former executive for software vendors, Ms. Miller has also held roles as Director of Finance, Controller and Business Office Manager in the provider environment. She has led numerous organizations through the process of defining a strategy, establishing measurement metrics, including expected ROI, building the operational support and processes to carry out the strategy and measuring the benefit achievement.

Table of Contents

List of Figures

List of Tables

Foreword

I remember the day in February 2003 that Pam Arlotto and her award-winning first book in the ROI series—*Return on Investment: Maximizing the Value of Healthcare Information Technology*—came into my life. I was attending my first HIMSS Conference, looking for ways to measure the benefits of health IT in my new role as Chief Medical Information Officer (CMIO) for the faculty group practice where I had worked since my medical school days.

I had previously been internal medicine residency director and had incorporated information technology to support residency education, administration, research, lifelong learning and certain aspects of patient care. While I found this highly rewarding, I was troubled by the sense that I could not provide these young physicians or their teachers with enough information management tools and skills to consistently deliver high-quality care to all patients during residency training and beyond. To do this better, we would need to digitize, organize and connect patient-specific information to knowledge resources, clinical decision support systems and data analytics tools. In short, we needed to move from paper charts to an electronic health record (EHR).

Of course, this was not a new idea. I had been advocating for EHR adoption in the practice since the Institute of Medicine's *The Computer-Based Patient Record: An Essential Technology for Health Care* was first published in 1991. I spent much of the next decade trying to convince others of the importance of implementing an EHR system, something that would be very hard to do without also being able to convince them that a financial return on investment (ROI) was not only possible but likely. With a paucity of published examples of positive financial ROI from EHR implementation and insufficient knowledge about what it would take to ensure and demonstrate a positive ROI, I struggled unsuccessfully to convince practice leaders to move the enterprise toward EHR adoption. However, one department was sufficiently convinced of the benefits and impatient for change that it courageously committed to investing its own financial and personnel resources, if needed, to implement a commercial EHR system for its clinic that, if successful, could be expanded to the rest of the practice.

My own patients had become accustomed to my ongoing commentary regarding the problems with paper-based medical records and my advocacy for adoption of EHR systems to support breakthrough improvements in healthcare quality and value. One patient, Michigan State University President M. Peter McPherson, was a particularly good listener and sounding board for my ideas in this area, as his banking and finance background, where IT had already transformed business practices, financial bottom lines and consumer engagement (think ATMs), made it easy for him to see the potential benefits of greater IT adoption in healthcare.

One of his visits with me took place at a particularly opportune time. He had just learned that there would be yet another large increase in university employee healthcare insurance costs for the coming year. He had read the Institute of Medicine reports *To Err is Human: Building a Safer Health System* and *Crossing the Quality Chasm: A New Health System for the 21st Century* that described the need for U.S. healthcare delivery system redesign and described the central importance of EHR systems to support needed improvements in quality and value. By the end of the conversation, he assigned me to lead the expansion of the EHR pilot from a single clinic to the entire faculty group practice and challenged me to demonstrate that the practice could leverage an EHR system to improve quality and generate savings.

I was now faced with a number of tasks. First, I needed to work with the CIO and EHR project team to ensure that we deployed a robust and reliable enterprise EHR that would support efforts to transform care quality and value. Second, since most of the costs of EHR implementation and ongoing use would be borne by clinical faculty as overhead costs, I needed to learn more about how to measure and improve savings and revenues in the transition from paper charts to electronic records.

An important challenge to change was the executive decision that no faculty salary support would be available to offset the expected decreases in clinical productivity during the transition to EHR use. This put us at serious risk of failure to adopt the EHR, so to help with physician engagement and continued willingness to strive for appropriate EHR use, I needed additional evidence that following our plan would yield sufficient efficiency gains to recoup the costs of EHR implementation in a reasonable timeframe and provide an ongoing savings on a go forward basis.

This is where Pam Arlotto's first ROI book was a treasure for me. While I was only able to glean a fraction of the wisdom at the time, I learned enough about how to measure ROI to set up a workable framework to use with colleagues. I learned about "payback period" methodology and found it to be a useful tool for demonstrating ROI in a way that was understandable and convincing to most providers and staff. I learned about the concept of "hard dollar" savings that I would need to rely on to convince even the most skeptical financial representatives in the practice that that EHR implementation and appropriate use was worth it from a financial perspective. Understanding that not all clinics were as far along in their EHR readiness or comfortable sharing their data on savings, I focused on studying the financial ROI in the internal medicine clinic where I was a provider and clinic director.

Using practice assessment tools and redesign strategies, combined with an intense focus on critical success factors for effective EHR implementation, internal medicine clinic providers and staff worked hard to use the EHR in a way that decreased waste and inefficiency. We reminded ourselves that our willingness to strive was rooted primarily in our desire to improve patient care quality and medical education rather than anticipated financial gains. We were hopeful our striving would also yield net benefits to our financial bottom line, but we would not be discouraged if such benefits were slow to accrue.

We used the principles articulated in the ROI book. We watched patiently as our hard dollar savings increased incrementally, while our monthly EHR costs remained stable. We were pleasantly surprised to see that we had recouped our entire EHR implementation costs 16.5 months following go-live, generating an average annual hard dollar savings of $63,000 per physician FTE during that time. We found this all the more remarkable in light of our high EHR initial ($44,767 per physician FTE) and annual maintenance costs ($12,761 per physician FTE). In the years since, we have sustained and expanded these financial gains while enjoying other benefits Pam and her colleagues predicted in her first and subsequent books in this series.

The timing of *Rethinking ROI: Accountable Meaningful Use* is impeccable. The book gives readers an opportunity to reflect on the enduring truths from the first two books for successful health IT adoption, change management and value realization. It also describes recent "game changers" such as ARRA/HITECH and the Affordable Care Act that are combining with other market forces to promote needed improvements in clinical quality, health information accessibility, provider effectiveness, operational efficiencies, patient engagement, population health management, care innovations and health information exchange. The book also contains valuable information for understanding and managing risk, measuring and monitoring performance, promoting clinical integration, ensuring effective organizational leadership and positioning healthcare organizations to thrive during a time of increasing accountability for quality and value.

Readers will find this book full of practical insights and helpful advice no matter where they are in their health IT adoption and care transformation journeys. Enjoy and be inspired.

Michael H. Zaroukian, MD, PhD, FACP, FHIMSS
Professor of Medicine, Michigan State University
Vice President and CMIO, Sparrow Health System

Chapter 1

Return on Investment: *A New Horizon*

Pam Arlotto

> *"To have lived through a revolution, to have seen a new birth of science, a new dispensation of health, reorganized medical schools, remodeled hospitals, a new outlook for humanity, is an opportunity not given to every generation."*
>
> Sir William Osler (1849–1919)

Does health information technology (IT) such as the electronic health record (EHR) have a return on investment (ROI)? This question has been debated at the highest levels of healthcare organizations for many years. For many, the ROI has been assumed; for others, the investment has been too great and progress has been slow. After exploring this concept for over a decade, the conclusion is the same. Technology alone does not drive ROI.

In 2007, the sequel to our first book, *Return on Investment: Maximizing the Value of Healthcare Information Technology*, expanded on our initial concept that ROI is part of a sophisticated value story in today's healthcare system. *Beyond Return on Investment: Expanding the Value of Healthcare Information Technology* depicted health IT as a strategic imperative for most healthcare enterprises—one that was essential in reducing medical errors, improving care efficiency and capturing market share. In both books, we defined value as "the degree of business and clinical performance improvement compared to the total IT and business investment."[1]

$$\text{Value of IT} = \frac{\text{Degree of Change in Business \& Clinical Outcomes}}{\text{Total IT \& Business Investment}}$$

1

With passage of the Health Information Technology for Economic and Clinical Health Act (HITECH) as part of the American Recovery and Reinvestment Act (ARRA) of 2009, the health IT landscape has changed. No longer focused on a single healthcare organization's deployment of clinical systems, the meaningful use of interoperable EHRs and other advanced clinical information technologies is foundational to our industry's shift to high-value healthcare. The ROI story is more crucial and complex than ever before.

The first book, *ROI: Maximizing the Value of Healthcare Information Technology* served as a basic primer or "how-to" on completing an ROI or value analysis for a single project or software application. The second book, *Beyond ROI: Expanding the Value of Healthcare Information Technology* provided a framework for the enterprise to realize the value of a portfolio of health IT projects and programs. This book shifts the focus to the meaningful use of EHRs—*To drive the transformation of the healthcare industry from volume- to value-based reimbursement, accountability and transparency through clinically integrated, patient-centered care* (see Figure 1-1).

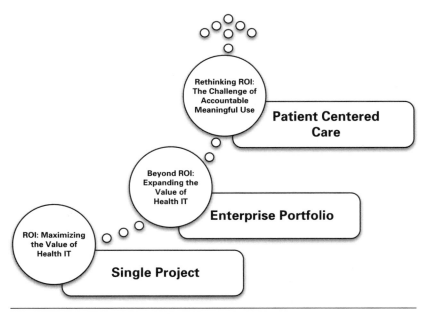

FIGURE 1-1: Evolution of ROI for Health IT.

A key message in this series is that, while much has changed, much remains the same. The adoption of EHRs by hospitals and physicians is increasing. However, most providers have yet to realize a return from their investment in these systems. A number of themes explaining why this is the case emerged in the first two books, and continues in this current edition, including:

- **Value must be managed into reality.** Many organizations estimate ROI or predict value as part of the budgeting process. Fewer continue to plan for, manage and measure value over the life of the investment. Ongoing value realization processes should be in place to ensure that benefits are realized.
- **Technology is a means to an end, not the ultimate goal.** Many organizations continue to focus on implementation of the EHR rather than how clinical systems align with and enable business strategies such as clinical integration, quality improvement and performance management.
- **Clinicians and healthcare business leaders must be accountable for value realization.** EHR deployments are more than IT projects—they are organizational change initiatives. Physicians must own and lead the change in care delivery redesign and standardization of clinical workflow. ROI and value realization are tied directly to outcomes improvement, patient safety and resource consumption. However, most clinicians have not been trained in performance improvement techniques. IT is often in the driver's seat, and value returns have been limited.
- **New governance structures and leadership skills are needed to drive transformation.** Medical staff committee structures, IT Steering Committees and Physician Advisory Groups, and traditional health system management structures were not designed to drive high-value healthcare. IT may "own" the information systems, but not the information or its impact on clinical care or the business of healthcare. As care delivery and reimbursement models change, new clinically integrated decision-making structures will be necessary to evaluate the meaning, use, policies and strategies to turn data into knowledge and action.
- **Value should be patient-centered.** Historically, we have focused on enterprise ROI and value realization. In the future, we must shift our thinking to an interoperable world, where data are exchanged across a

community, region, state and possibly the nation. Coordination of care
and cross-venue quality measurement will drive value creation. New
reimbursement models will create incentives to move from provider-
centric to patient-centered care, creating a new definition of ROI.

Dramatic changes are on the horizon that may result in industry consolidation, reengineering and the closure of some entities. Because of the
impending upheaval, we must *rethink* ROI. In the past, value realization was an internal decision—a journey that could be paced over years,
allowing for trial and error. Today, the pace of change has accelerated and
Meaningful Use compliance requires external transparency. Meaningful
Use incentive payments only cover one quarter to one third of the investment required to fully deploy and optimize EHRs and advanced clinical
systems. No longer optional, ROI and value realization will be necessary
to survive in the healthcare delivery system of the future. Reimbursement
will be based on the provision of value and the ability to demonstrate
outcomes improvement.

This book helps readers *rethink* their definition of the ROI of health
IT. It sets the stage by exploring the intent of the HITECH legislation
and explores Meaningful Use as a value realization strategy—one that is
foundational to healthcare reform. Over the past decade, health IT leaders have concluded that ROI analysis and tracking takes too much time.
Given limited resources, the investment to measure the return has been
too great. In this book, we provide a streamlined Value Management
Framework which focuses on measurement during three stages: value
identification, value realization and value optimization. The approach
encourages multidisciplinary teams to understand the value levers of
Meaningful Use and the opportunity to create strategic value unique
to their health system. Planning for value is emphasized, as well as integrated into governance, process redesign, adoption management and IT
implementation.

A significant portion of the book is dedicated to specific value vignettes
depicting value maps for benefits such as quality improvement, care
management, cost reduction etc. The benefits are examined within the
context of Meaningful Use. Key metrics, processes, accountabilities and
technologies for value realization are described to give the reader a guide to
customizing the realization of return on investment for their organization.

Finally, a ten-year perspective is provided. If we successfully realize the
value of health IT, where will it take us? Time will tell.

Chapter 2

Accountable Meaningful Use

Pam Arlotto

> *"The provisions of the HITECH Act are best understood not as investments in technology per se but as efforts to improve the health of Americans and the performance of their health care system."*
>
> David Blumenthal, MD, MPP, Former National Coordinator for
> Health Information Technology[2]

The Patient Protection and Affordable Care Act (PPACA, the Affordable Care Act or ACA) of 2010 has its supporters and detractors. Whether implemented completely, modified or repealed, providers must acknowledge that the rate of healthcare spending is unsustainable. Rather than following the traditional course of "waiting for the other shoe to drop" prior to action, proactive healthcare organizations are transforming into high-value healthcare delivery systems for the future.

The primary lever that will drive this transformation is Value Based Purchasing (VBP). Initially, providers will experience deep cuts in reimbursement. Over the longer term, payers will move from fee for service to bundled or population-based payments. VBP is a methodology that rewards quality of care through payment incentives and transparency. In VBP, providers are held accountable for the quality and cost of the healthcare services they provide by a system of rewards and consequences, conditional upon achieving pre-specified performance measures. Additionally, incentives are structured to discourage inappropriate, unnecessary and costly care.[3] While closely tied with ACA, the Centers for Medicare & Medicaid Services (CMS) began implementing VBP demonstration projects as early as 2003. In addition, commercial payers have been piloting pay-for-performance for some time. Regardless of ACA's destiny, VBP at some level will drive transformation of the healthcare industry.

There will be a number of transitions healthcare organizations must make to prepare for the move to value-based healthcare. At the core of the transformation is *clinical integration*[4]—a strategy that many agree is inevitable.

Clinical integration will be enabled through a shared EHR, point of care clinical guidelines, disease management programs and a new patient-centered culture. Each patient's healthcare needs will be evaluated and treated comprehensively as part of a system of care for that person. The result is patient care that is coordinated across all conditions, diseases, providers and care venues, over time. The goal is to achieve optimal results in efficiency, cost, safety and timing, as well as overall quality of care.[5] In other words, the goal is improved *value* for both the patient and the payer.

> ***Clinical integration*** is defined as the extent to which patient care services are coordinated across people, functions, activities, processes and operating units so as to maximize the value of services delivered. Clinical integration includes both horizontal integration (the coordination of activities at the same stage of delivery of care) as well as vertical integration (the coordination of services at different stages).
>
> **Stephen M. Shortell, PhD., MPH**

Additionally, care must become patient-centered. Vaulted into the spotlight in 2001 by the Institute of Medicine's (IOM) publication *Crossing the Quality Chasm*,[6] patient-centered care (PCC) is at the heart of the quality and patient safety discussion and is foundational to most proposed reform initiatives. Specifically, PCC provides a system of care that explores the patient's main reason for the visit, concerns and need for information; seeks an integrated understanding of the patient's world—that is, the individual as a whole person, with emotional needs and life issues; finds common ground on what the problem is and mutually agrees on management; encourages prevention and health promotion;

and enhances the continuing relationship between the patient and the physician.[7]

VBP, Clinical Integration and PCC will require standardized, comparative and transparent information on patient outcomes, healthcare status, and patient experience and costs (both direct and indirect) of services provided.[8] According to CEO of Siemens Health Services, John Glaser, "One really ought to assume that HITECH is fundamentally laying the foundation for payment and structural reform, which assumes widespread meaningful use of interoperable EHRs…*Meaningful Use becomes the tactical plan for achieving the strategic plan outlined by ACA*".[9]

Meaningful Use will be staged in at least three steps over the course of the next five years. It should be noted that each stage builds on the progress made during the prior stage, as shown in Figure 2-1.

Prior to the creation of the Meaningful Use criteria and standards, the Markle Foundation proposed a simple definition of patient-centered, meaningful use of health IT: providers make use of, and the patient has access to, clinically relevant electronic information about the patient to improve patient outcomes and health status, to improve the delivery of

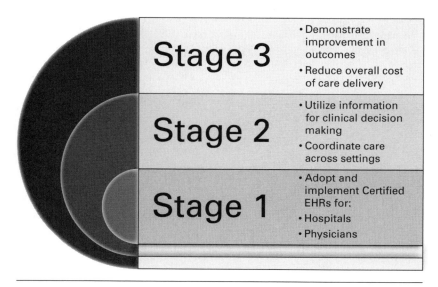

Figure 2-1: Stages of Meaningful Use.

care and to control the growth of costs.[10] For this to occur, healthcare providers must recognize that technology alone will not realign, redesign or reengineer healthcare. As new healthcare delivery and payment models emerge, industry leaders must *rethink* the desired results and the approach to achieving them.

Traditionally, healthcare leaders built health IT business cases focused on tactical savings from streamlining staffing (full-time equivalents), reducing supply costs or eliminating errors. In the future, these tactical savings will not be enough to justify purchase and implementation of technology. The Economic Value Pathway (Figure 2-2) depicts a full spectrum of quantitative and qualitative value that can be realized from a combined investment in health IT and patient care redesign. As one moves from a tactical perspective to a more strategic focus on redesign of care delivery and reimbursement models, the magnitude of potential benefits expand.[11]

In order to rethink the desired results, we must begin to redefine healthcare as a series of cross-venue processes. Historically, healthcare providers have been structured according to functional departments or specialties within the confines of hospitals, physician practices, ambulatory clinics, rehabilitation facilities, long-term care and home health/hospice organizations. In high-value healthcare, patient-centered processes that cross the care continuum will be standardized. Decision support tools and quality metrics will drive multidisciplinary care teams as they care for

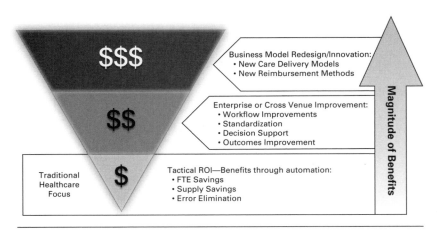

FIGURE 2-2: Economic Value Pathway.

patients and hold themselves accountable for the resources used, delivery costs incurred and for outcomes produced.

VBP is expected to reduce Medicare spending by approximately $214 billion over the next 10 years.[12] The implications are significant to hospitals and physicians. A planned shift to prevention and away from acute care will lead to consolidation and closure of many facilities. Existing organizations will be forced to reinvent their business models. "Accountability" for system performance will be the prime directive for those in healthcare. Healthcare providers will shift the emphasis from caring for one patient at a time to managing health for a defined population of patients.[13]

The successful healthcare organization of the future has already begun to rethink its own value proposition and the role health IT will play in achieving the value proposition in the accountable future. Meaningful Use must be combined with development of new decision-making structures to ensure that the EHR does more than automate the paper record. Value will only be realized if the EHR is aligned with a Transformation Strategy that has specific goals. Key principles guiding the strategy must include:

- Care is patient-centered and coordinated across provider venues, not just focused on acute episodes such as inpatient encounters.
- Systematized processes are developed and driven by evidence-based medicine to reduce variation in practice.
- Transparent operations will ensure clear authority and responsibility for point of care decision making.
- Patients are involved in their own care, understand the value of wellness and prevention and have access to care providers.
- Metrics are developed for key outcomes to drive performance improvement and value realization.

According to Vice President of Regional Health Information Organization Development at AtlantiCare, Daniel Morreale, "Meaningful Use will separate the haves and have-nots. Those organizations that survive will achieve alignment in strategy, quality, the physician community and finances. The others will fall by the wayside due to poor quality, inability to engage physicians and inadequate finances."[14] Healthcare organizations typically fall into one of four categories in their approach to Meaningful Use, as shown in Figure 2-3.

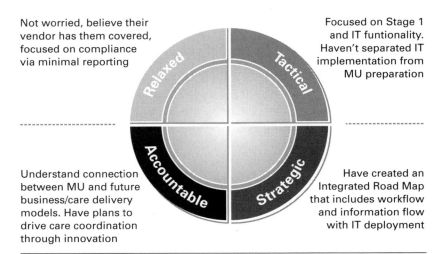

Not worried, believe their vendor has them covered, focused on compliance via minimal reporting

Focused on Stage 1 and IT funtionality. Haven't separated IT implementation from MU preparation

Understand connection between MU and future business/care delivery models. Have plans to drive care coordination through innovation

Have created an Integrated Road Map that includes workflow and information flow with IT deployment

FIGURE 2-3: Strategic Approaches to Meaningful Use.

These categories can be further described as follows:

- **Relaxed**—These organizations are not worried. They have confidence in their health IT vendor, to a fault. They feel they are implementing "certified electronic health record" technology, and they will do just enough to get by. These health systems have bought into a common misperception—that implementing EHR technology automatically demonstrates Meaningful Use.
- **Tactical**—Many organizations are approaching Meaningful Use as a tactical endeavor. They are heads down with their focus on Stage 1. Leadership has not looked over the horizon to make sure they lay the foundation for future stages. They have a clinical system application plan but have not developed a plan for Meaningful Use. While they recognize the mutual responsibilities of the vendor and provider, they only view Meaningful Use from the perspective of technology implementation.
- **Strategic**—Health systems at this level view information technology as a strategic asset. They understand that successful Meaningful Use of EHRs is not an IT project but an organizational change project. These health systems have created an integrated road map that includes workflow and information flow redesign prior to implementation of systems. Wary of automating broken processes, they spend resources and time for thoughtful planning and invest heavily in clinical informatics, process redesign and project management.

- **Accountable**—For these organizations, the future of healthcare is focused on using information in new and different ways to redesign care delivery and reimbursement models across venues of care. While only a few organizations are planning for the *Accountable* Meaningful Use of EHRs, they serve as the standard for the entire industry. These organizations are forward-looking and are designing evidence-based systems of care, providing clinical decision support at the point of care and turning data into knowledge by aggregating information, reporting to key care givers and changing the way they deliver care in order to better manage patient populations and positively influence outcomes.[15]

> ## Over 50% of US hospitals are relaxed or tactical
>
> *(Source: Maestro Strategies MU Readiness Assessments and Surveys)*

As Donald Berwick states, "healthcare is hungry for something truly new, less a fad than a new way to be."[16] No longer about the value and ROI of health IT, the future is about innovative, patient-centered care teams that use information from the EHR and other systems to drive value out of a newly designed healthcare system. So a new bar has been raised: organizations can step up to Accountable Meaningful Use and proactively design in value to ensure the optimal return on their investment in their information technology dollars.

Chapter 3

Improving Value through Accountable Meaningful Use: *A Framework*

Pam Arlotto

> *"Value in any field must be defined around the customer, not the supplier. Value must also be measured by outputs, not inputs. Hence it is patient health results that matter, not the volume of services delivered."*
>
> Michael Porter, Harvard Business School

Within the HITECH Act, which was enacted as part of ARRA, it was clearly stated that the objective of Meaningful Use is the improvement of healthcare quality (outcomes, efficiency, safety and service), not merely the adoption of health IT. As illustrated in the previous chapter's Strategic Approaches to Meaningful Use diagram (Figure 2-3), for many organizations, Meaningful Use has become an exercise of technology implementation and compliance for the purpose of capturing stimulus dollars rather than an opportunity to drive healthcare delivery redesign.

The intent of the Meaningful Use legislation was to improve healthcare quality and outcomes. The specific goals that can be extrapolated from the Meaningful Use requirements are to:

- Reduce hospital readmissions.
- Improve medication management (safe medication use and effective medication management for heart disease, diabetes, asthma, mental health conditions and hospital procedures).
- Improve care coordination and reduce gaps in care.
- Improve chronic care management, including blood pressure, diabetes and cholesterol control.

- Improve preventative care, including healthy weight and smoking cessation.
- Improve patient safety.
- Reduce disparities in care delivery.
- Increase efficiency and appropriate use of resources.
- Improve active engagement of patients in their care.[17]

As an example, further examination of the patient engagement goal demonstrates a staged path to PCC through Meaningful Use. Figure 3-1 describes the fundamental tenets of Patient-Centered Care and links them to the technologies/objectives included in Meaningful Use.

Within the scope of High-Value Healthcare, Meaningful Use becomes embedded in the delivery of quality outcomes and the total cost of care. In other words, healthcare organizations will not be able to transition to the healthcare delivery and reimbursement system of the future without addressing the Meaningful Use imperative. Value should be managed during each stage of Meaningful Use to ensure ROI and attainment of strategic benefit. Leaders should be assigned accountability for driving results, benefits and outcomes. This chapter provides a Value Management Framework for use when developing Accountable Meaningful Use mitigation plans.

$$\text{High Value Healthcare} = \frac{\textbf{Quality}\ (\textit{Outcomes, Efficiency, Safety, Service})}{\textbf{Total Cost of Care}}$$

Health IT Portfolio Investment Requirements

Historically, health systems have developed IT capital budgets on a year-to-year basis against a high-level IT strategy that included a mix of strategic, routine, mandated and tactical projects. Most organizations focused on one major strategic application at a time (e.g., revenue cycle management, supply chain or computerized physician order entry [CPOE]). Routine requests for departmental systems or infrastructure upgrades tended to consume the bulk of the IT investment.

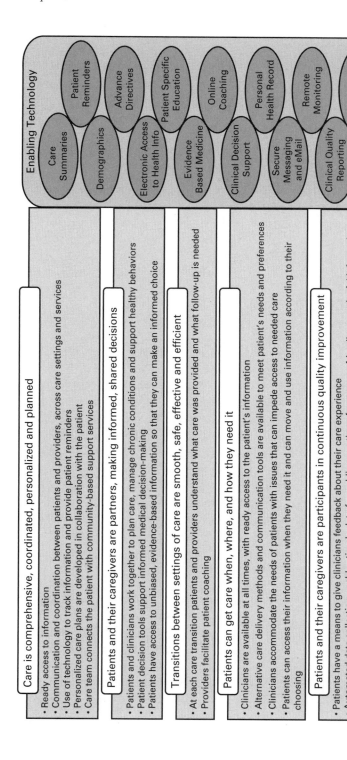

Enabling Technology

Care Summaries · Patient Reminders · Demographics · Advance Directives · Electronic Access to Health Info · Patient Specific Education · Evidence Based Medicine · Online Coaching · Clinical Decision Support · Personal Health Record · Secure Messaging and eMail · Remote Monitoring · Clinical Quality Reporting · Patient-Reported Quality · Cost and Outcomes Reporting

Care is comprehensive, coordinated, personalized and planned
- Ready access to information
- Communication and coordination between patients and providers, across care settings and services
- Use of technology to track information and provide patient reminders
- Personalized care plans are developed in collaboration with the patient
- Care team connects the patient with community-based support services

Patients and their caregivers are partners, making informed, shared decisions
- Patients and clinicians work together to plan care, manage chronic conditions and support healthy behaviors
- Patient decision tools support informed medical decision-making
- Patients have access to unbiased, evidence-based information so that they can make an informed choice

Transitions between settings of care are smooth, safe, effective and efficient
- At each care transition patients and providers understand what care was provided and what follow-up is needed
- Providers facilitate patient coaching

Patients can get care when, where, and how they need it
- Clinicians are available at all times, with ready access to the patient's information
- Alternative care delivery methods and communication tools are available to meet patient's needs and preferences
- Clinicians accommodate the needs of patients with issues that can impede access to needed care
- Patients can access their information when they need it and can move and use information according to their choosing

Patients and their caregivers are participants in continuous quality improvement
- Patients have a means to give clinicians feedback about their care experience
- Automated data collection enables timely data for public reporting of consumer-friendly, meaningful information about cost and quality of care
- Quality and cost information is used by consumers to choose their care providers, as well as to inform patients about standards of care
- Patients are involved in the redesign of care delivery processes

FIGURE 3-1: Technologies Supporting Patient-Centered Care.

Meaningful Use has had a dramatic impact on the IT portfolio investment strategy of most organizations because:

- The federal government has designed the health IT strategy for most organizations and their vendor partners.
- Many clinical applications and modules must be implemented simultaneously.
- Physicians must adopt health IT solutions and for many, this is their first involvement.
- The bulk of the enterprise's capital dollars must now be dedicated to Meaningful Use, and other projects are delayed or cancelled.
- Timelines are less flexible and in fact are dictated in part by the legislation—as well as vendor timelines to provide certified applications and associated implementation support.
- More clinical resources are required both within IT and in care delivery areas to design new clinical workflows in which technology is imbedded.
- Organizations must be prepared to maintain adoption levels by monitoring thresholds associated with Meaningful Use on a regular basis.

Now, Meaningful Use has become the sole investment focus of many health systems and provider organizations. Operational or departmental systems improvements or selections have been virtually abandoned. "Back-office" or infrastructure projects are still important, but the risks associated with delaying or not investing have been greatly diminished given the rising significance of Meaningful Use. Investments in innovative use of information technologies to drive new approaches to healthcare delivery, competitive advantage or future performance are often not considered. Many organizations feel the risks and investment are too high for experimentation (see Figure 3-2).

The required investment for Meaningful Use goes far beyond software and hardware. The most significant investment needed will be in the development of the *organizational capacity for transformation*.[19] Beyond current capabilities in care delivery and IT, additional skilled resources will be needed to redesign care processes, develop evidence-based systems of care, mine data and convert them into useful information for decision makers, manage large sophisticated projects, etc. Building this organizational capacity will take time and significant investment. It is widely recognized that incentive payments for hospitals and eligible providers will cover only 20–25 percent of the overall cost to implement an

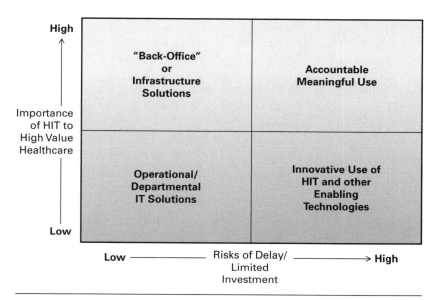

F<small>IGURE</small> 3-2: New Health IT Portfolio.[18]

Organizational capacity is simply defined as the organization's ability to perform. Accountable MU will require investment in organizational capacity (expertise) in planning, new decision-making structures, project management, clinical and medical informatics, process redesign, change management, knowledge management, decision support and analytics, communications, measurement and system implementation to improve its ability to perform in the high-value healthcare enterprise of the future.

EHR and achieve Meaningful Use.[20] Other estimates demonstrate the "breath-taking" nature of this investment.

Hospitals
- A complete EHR for a 500-bed hospital will take $50 million and at least four years.[21]
- Average start-up cost per bed is $80,000–$100,000 (200 beds).[22]
- Most hospitals underestimate by 100 percent average cost to implement EHR.[23]

Physicians

- The average cost of a practice EHR ranges from $55,000 to $200,000 per physician.[24]

Health Information Exchange (HIE)

- Major vendors charge $20,000 to $50,000 for just their side of an admission, discharge, transfer (ADT) interface.[25] Additional interfaces to be considered include (but are not limited to) lab, radiology, pharmacy and surgery.
- Average cost per physician practice to interface to one "trading partner" is $19,000.

No longer optional, ROI and value realization is the go-forward strategy for healthcare organizations to survive and thrive. *Value does not happen without a plan.* In the past, many healthcare providers assumed health IT was a "cost of doing business." If ROI was calculated, it was often conducted using a discrete cost-benefit analysis focused solely on the technology. Some organizations used more sophisticated business case evaluations that considered tangible and intangible benefits, as well as identifying direct and indirect costs in order to compute more sophisticated metrics such as cash flow, cost-benefit ratios, payback period, net present value and internal rate of return.[26] Typically these methods focused on justifying acquisition of health IT rather than ensuring that value was realized throughout the life of the project.

As the industry transitions to high-value healthcare, value realization must be proactively planned for, managed and optimized. A formal value management process that identifies the desired benefits early and builds them into detailed project plans—coupled with an increased focus on business results, is critical to achieving Meaningful Use.

Research conducted by the London School of Economics-McKinsey offers evidence that, regardless of an organizations' location, industry, size or historical performance, improvement in management practices in conjunction with IT implementation results in dramatically improved performance as shown in Figure 3-3.[27]

While many in healthcare have adopted the mantra—Meaningful Use is more than an IT project; it is an organizational change project— few have taken it one step further, by adopting value management

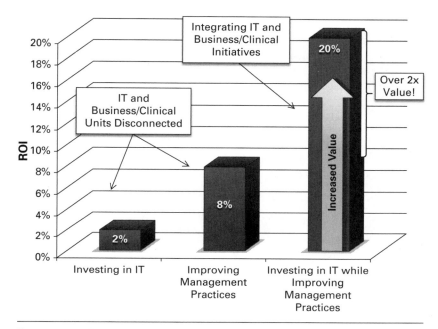

F<small>IGURE</small> 3-3: Value Realization—IT Only v. IT and Improved Management Practices (e.g., process redesign, change management and performance measurement).

strategies to execute projects consistently and drive aggressive returns. These value management strategies include detailed value discovery and planning, governance and decision-making structures, process redesign, metrics management and change management—all of which impact the organizational capacity needed for delivering high-value healthcare.

We have identified four levels of IT value management maturity as illustrated in Figure 3-4. The first level, "Cost of Doing Business," is the most immature and has little or no process improvement associated with the IT deployment. The fourth level, "Value Management" is the most mature, and has integrated IT value realization into the transformation plan. According to surveys conducted to evaluate Value Management best practice, 75 percent of organizations that use mature value management practices realize their value targets on-time or early, 42 percent meet their targets and an additional 19 percent exceed their value targets.[28]

	Cost of Doing Business	Cost-Benefit Analysis	Formal Business Case Justification	Value Management
Value Identification	■ No benefit quantification ■ No linkage to strategic initiatives ■ Assume benefits will automatically happen	■ High level quantification of costs and benefits ■ Informal linkage to strategic initiatives	■ Business case is defined in advance of system selection ■ Costs and benefits are identified one-time in advance of implementation ■ Key metrics are identified ■ Alignment of strategic initiatives and business case ■ "Hard" ROI hurdle rate is often used	■ Value is identified and planned at each stage of the project life cycle ■ Business or clinical value is the end goal, not IT value ■ Formal relationship between strategic initiatives and value realization goals ■ Value includes quantitative and qualitative metrics ■ Accountability for value realization is assigned
Level of Transformation	■ Little or no process change	■ Incremental process change focused on automation of existing processes	■ Moderate level of process change through best practice integration	■ Significant level of process change, innovation or transformation
Measurement	■ No value measurement	■ Value assessment is anecdotal	■ Value is tracked through IT project related performance metrics	■ Value is realized and optimized through ongoing tracking and improvement

FIGURE 3-4: IT Value Management Maturity Model.

Many organizations are tempted to short-circuit formal value management techniques and approaches—assuming that the ROI will become evident over time. However, without a structured process, one of three things can happen:

- The technology becomes the focus which leads to limited impact on value.
- Aspiration does not translate into performance.
- Broken processes, organization structures and culture derail even the most sophisticated software solutions.

Successful healthcare organizations—the "winners" in High-Value Healthcare, will have to move beyond the first three levels of value management maturity and focus on the top tier of the Value Management construct where they must identify value, transform the organization and demonstrate success through measurement and reporting of outcomes. Value cannot be left on the table or assumed, or only used to justify systems. Value must be planned for, realized and optimized.

A Framework for Value Management

Value Management will become a critical discipline for healthcare organizations. Deliberate, results-focused methods that drive outcomes must become standard operating practice and part of the very DNA of high performing healthcare provider organizations. Given the resource constrained environment of healthcare today, a modified, streamlined approach to Value Management is needed. The Value Management Framework described next and in the following three chapters, provides an approach to:

- Focus the attention of key leaders, program managers and clinicians on leveraging technology and process change for value improvement.
- Insert value measurement into strategy development, stakeholder awareness, road map planning, project management, process redesign and system implementation.
- Disseminate value optimization tools throughout the care delivery and transformation team.
- Integrate the Value Management process with Meaningful Use mitigation planning activities to ensure Accountable Meaningful Use.

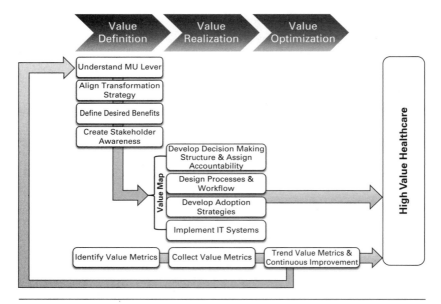

FIGURE 3-5: Value Management Framework.

There are three stages of a successful Value Management process, as outlined in Figure 3-5:

- **Value Definition**—Understanding the problem you are trying to solve, identifying the associated Meaningful Use value lever and developing a plan to realize value with key Transformation Strategies.
- **Value Realization**—Focusing on value delivery, designing standardized, "hard-wired" processes, creating adoption plans and implementing key health IT systems.
- **Value Optimization**—Using value metrics identified during the Value Definition phase, collecting key indicators during the Value Realization phase and analyzing results during the Value Optimization Phase provides an ongoing feedback loop for continuous improvement and transformation.

Chapters 4, 5 and 6 provide more detail about the Value Definition, Value Realization and Value Optimization components of the Value Management Framework. Value maps are provided around a number of example strategies and Meaningful Use levers.

Chapter 4

Value Definition

Pam Arlotto and Susan Irby

"We believe that physicians and healthcare leaders are in a key position to implement meaningful change that makes care safer, more efficient, more effective, and more attuned to each patient's needs and preferences. At the same time, based on our research and individual experience, we know that by doing this, we actually lower cost."

James N. Weinstein, MS, DO, Director of the Dartmouth Institute &
President of the Dartmouth-Hitchcock Clinic

The first phase of developing the Value Management Framework is Value Definition. Rather than spending many hours planning and debating specific strategies and benefit goals, teams can meet quickly to discuss and define the goals of Accountable Meaningful Use relative to their organization and the value they hope to achieve. In this chapter, the reader will be able to:

- Understand the Meaningful Use Value Levers.
- Align Transformation Strategy.
- Define Desired Benefits.
- Create Stakeholder Awareness.
- Develop Value Maps.

Eleven examples of Value Maps are depicted at the end of Chapter 4.

Understand the Meaningful Use Value Levers

Meaningful Use was designed to *leverage* the EHR and other advanced clinical technologies in order to create value. In other words, Meaningful Use is foundational to high-value healthcare, not because of the technology, but because of the ability to inform providers as they increase preventative care, manage chronic diseases more efficiently and effectively, coordinate care across the continuum, create new models of care and incorporate the use of evidence-based medicine.

The first step in the Value Definition phase of the Value Management Process is to understand the *value levers* of Meaningful Use. The Collins English Dictionary defines a lever as *a means of exerting pressure in order to accomplish something; a strategic aid.*[29] Health systems should apply both components of this definition toward their progress toward Meaningful Use. Specifically, organizations should:

- Recognize the external pressure from CMS and other payers to meet Meaningful Use criteria for the purpose of driving reimbursement changes (see Figure 4-1).
- Customize strategies associated with Meaningful Use and accountable care to create value unique to each health system's environment.

Each eligible hospital and eligible provider will be measured against specific thresholds, EHR certification standards and core/menu requirements. Ultimately, as Meaningful Use progresses, providers will be evaluated on the way they use the EHR information from the patient and the provider to capture, analyze and improve decisions regarding diagnosis, care plans and treatments.

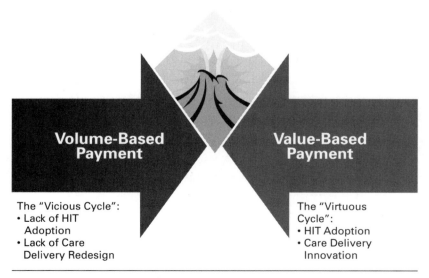

FIGURE 4-1: Drivers for Meaningful Use.

For example, one Meaningful Use value lever is the maintenance of an "up-to-date problem list of current and active diagnoses." Based on the problem-centered approach to care delivery, and defined over 40 years ago in the seminal *New England Journal of Medicine* article, was the concept of the problem-oriented medical record, developed by Lawrence Weed, MD.[30] In its most optimized form, the problem list provides physicians, care team members, medical coders and others a complete, concise and clinically accurate view of the patient's health status. Inclusion in Meaningful Use Stage 1, and expansion of requirements over future stages, demonstrates the need to standardize the creation and management of an accessible problem list to drive integrated, clinical care across multiple provider sites.

In order to fully understand each Meaningful Use requirement and its use as a value lever, one needs to:

- Review the history and purpose of the Meaningful Use criteria.
- Understand its function pre-automation.
- Understand how the EHR can or should be applied.
- Uncover best practices related to the creation of value.
- Identify the workflow, training and information impact.
- Examine the investment required to realize specific benefits.
- Review typical barriers and unintended consequences.
- Discuss options for roll-out with key stakeholders.
- Understand timing, cost and alternative staging opportunities.

For most organizations, these steps can be done rather quickly. In order to realize value and produce results, best practice research should be conducted; leadership should ask these questions and others to ensure they fully understand the minimum requirements to comply with basic Meaningful Use, as well as the opportunities to create strategic value unique to the organization.

Align Transformation Strategy

Once the organization has a complete understanding of the Meaningful Use value lever, they should connect Meaningful Use requirements to key enterprise strategic initiatives. For years, IT thought leaders encouraged Chief Information Officers (CIOs) to link IT strategy with enterprise strategy. Strategic planning is an iterative process that ensures all parts of the organization are working together to reach common goals. Meaningful Use plans should be integrated not only with IT Strategy, but to support enterprise strategy. Leaders within organizations should be able to assess Meaningful Use, its impact on the strategic imperatives of the organization and be able to:

- Understand the big picture perspective and the problems/challenges of the healthcare industry today.
- Consider healthcare transformation trends and the potential impact on acute care, ambulatory care and other aspects of the healthcare delivery system.
- Identify key stakeholders within the organization and within the community.
- Ascertain political agendas and adjust decisions and actions accordingly.
- Appreciate the pressures faced by key stakeholders.
- Synthesize information, understand the interrelationships between issues and recognize causal relationships.
- Be aware of the upstream and downstream effects of key decisions.
- View strategies from different perspectives and points of view.
- Identify common elements or trends in situations and actions.
- Ensure decisions are made at the right level.
- Provide decision makers with appropriate research and information.
- Customize the decisions to the specific needs of the organization.
- Break down each strategy into a practical performance plan.

Alignment with overall strategic direction and key strategic initiatives will guide leadership in developing the detailed plans around each Meaningful Use value lever. Using the problem list as an example, if an organization has a strategy around the Patient Centered Medical Home (PCMH), deployment of the problem list as part of the value realization plan might include customization of workflows, policies and protocols. In the PCMH, the primary care physician (PCP) serves as the coordinator of care, and accountability for updating the problem list can be assigned to each patient's PCP. Using a shared problem list, specialists can recommend additions to the comprehensive list and health profile. Removal of problems would be at the discretion of the primary care provider in consultation with the patient and other authorized caregivers.[31] Organizations without this strategy may prefer to use nurse case managers to ensure that problem lists are up-to-date and maintained.

Another strategic alignment example for this value lever is in the area of health information exchange (HIE). HIE strategy should be closely tied to clinical integration and care coordination strategies. The Continuity of Care Document standard developed by the American Society for Testing and Materials (ASTM) includes a data segment for problem lists. Problem list deployment and management across multiple entities have its own set of challenges and decisions. Health systems are choosing a variety of approaches to integrate with physicians, including employment, physician-hospital organizations, clinical institutes, co-management and other models. The aggressiveness and approach to each strategy will depend on a number of factors including competitive positioning of the organization, volume-based payments versus value-based purchasing environment, clinician readiness, organization capacity, etc.

Figure 4-2 depicts Meaningful Use objectives and their alignment with key strategic initiatives.

Define Desired Benefits

The fundamental reason for Meaningful Use and investment in new technologies is benefit realization. Using the information gained in the previous two sections will allow an organization to clarify its desired end state. It is important not to confuse Meaningful Use thresholds with the desired end state. The purpose of demonstrating meeting various thresholds in Stage 1 is to demonstrate successful implementation and use of system functionality, as opposed to immediately impacting outcomes. Recent research conducted by RAND determined that Stage 1 Meaningful Use thresholds for hospitals requiring use of electronic orders for at least 30 percent of eligible patients is probably too low to have a significant impact on deaths from heart failure and heart attack among hospitalized Medicare beneficiaries. However, the proposed threshold for the next stage of the program—using the orders for at least 60 percent of patients, (a rate some stakeholders have said is too high) is more consistently associated with lower mortality.[32] Therefore, it is important for leadership to determine whether their overall benefit goal is: 1) compliance only, or 2) value improvement.

Additionally, decision makers should explore the impact of and investment required to achieve alternative future states. This discovery process helps identify and eventually prioritize desired results. Questions organizations should ask include:

- What are similar organizations doing? Similar can be defined by region, by vendor, by size, by level of adoption or innovation, etc.
- Has the organization engaged in a similar change initiative? What were the results? What were the lessons learned?

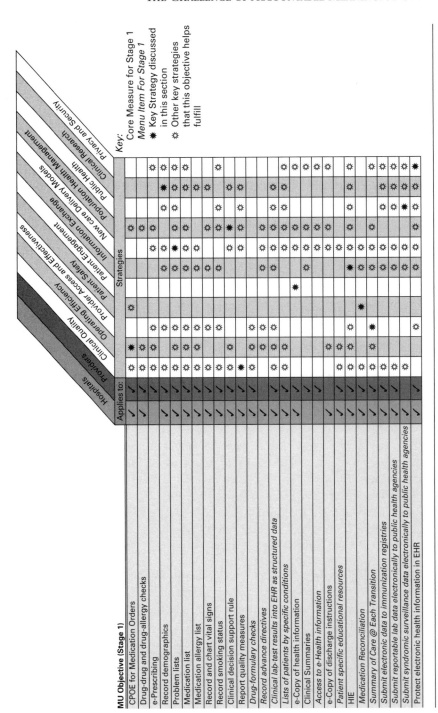

FIGURE 4-2: Meaningful Use Objectives and Strategies.

- Who are the direct and indirect stakeholders? What do they desire for the organization?
- What are the immediate consolidation, integration or information sharing plans of the organization? Who else will this impact?
- What is the organization's standing in the community—today and tomorrow? What standing does the organization wish to have in the future?
- What are the risks associated with this initiative?
- What tools, technologies and resources are required to create the future state?
- What are the major barriers?

Returning to the problem list example, an optimized problem list can produce benefits associated with care coordination, cost accountability and clinical effectiveness. It is up to each organization to expand on, further define the desired value and prioritize the specific benefits. The problem list can identify the most important health factors for each patient and groupings of disease-specific populations. This information can be used to produce the following benefits:

- Increases in the number of patients with customized care plans.
- Increases in the development of disease-specific protocols.
- Improved outcome performance.
- Increases in the number of patients receiving preventative care.
- Improved effectiveness of chronic care interventions.
- Increases in the use of healthcare enterprise or individual practitioner score cards.
- Increases in patients screened for clinical research studies.
- Improved patient assessments.
- Reduced workflow inefficiencies and medical errors.
- Reduced duplication of diagnostic and interventional procedures, eliminating waste and preventing unnecessary care.

Ultimately, the benefits related to Meaningful Use for an organization and for a community will have to be prioritized and further quantified. Some are early stage benefits and others are later stage benefits. The level of detail required to define benefits will vary based on the magnitude of the benefit, as well as the areas across which the benefit may apply. Initially, organizations will want to focus on a short list of the benefits to determine short-term, intermediate- and long-term impact on the transformation initiative deliverables.

Create Stakeholder Awareness

Generally, there are four ways IT can bring value to an enterprise (see Figure 4-3). None of the four is preferred over the others, and most organizations will use all of the four at one time or another. Often value created in one quadrant leads to value created in another quadrant. It is, however, essential that key stakeholders understand the opportunities, weigh in on their value and participate in the steps toward value realization.[33]

John Kotter, a professor at Harvard Business School and world-renowned change expert, suggests that for an organization to be successful in its change efforts, 75 percent of a company's management needs to "buy into" the change. In other words, for Meaningful Use and value realization of EHRs to be successful, organizations need to create a sense of urgency regarding the potential results. There are two distinct perspectives on the tone of the urgency: 1) the threat-based approach—"if we don't do it, what will be the negative impact," and 2) the opportunity-based approach—"if we do it, what will be the positive result?" In the current environment, we find compliance-based organizations aligning with the first messaging and value-based organizations preferring the more positive positioning.

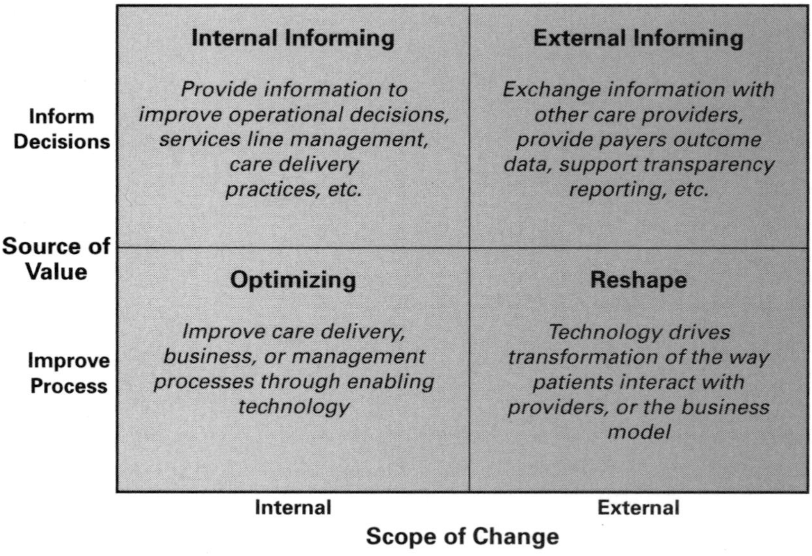

	Internal Informing	**External Informing**
Inform Decisions	*Provide information to improve operational decisions, services line management, care delivery practices, etc.*	*Exchange information with other care providers, provide payers outcome data, support transparency reporting, etc.*
Source of Value		
	Optimizing	**Reshape**
Improve Process	*Improve care delivery, business, or management processes through enabling technology*	*Technology drives transformation of the way patients interact with providers, or the business model*
	Internal	**External**
	Scope of Change	

FIGURE 4-3: Value Quadrants.

Stakeholder groups should be segmented by readiness, specialty or level within the organization and a variety of other factors. A communications plan should be developed for each segment. Important questions to answer include:

- What messages do you want to convey to the group?
- What is the current status of each segment and the individual stakeholders within that segment?
- What are current expectations?
- What are the group's current objectives and issues?
- Does the group advocate, support, criticize, block or prefer to be neutral?
- Who are the leaders within the group?
- What actions are desired?
- What investments are needed?
- How will the segment and leadership recognize success?

These questions will support the development of specific communication strategies for each segment. Each strategy can be broken down into a series of small, achievable steps and actions that can be addressed one by one.

Develop Value Maps

Management theorist Russell Ackoff once said, "A problem never exists in isolation; it is surrounded by other problems. The more of the context of a problem that a leader can comprehend, the greater are the chances of finding a truly adequate solution."[34] Value Mapping is a technique that focuses multidisciplinary discussion around the interrelated steps of the planning, execution and continuous improvement aspects of a transformation initiative.

Derived from Lean methods, the purpose of the Value Map is not the map itself, but to provide a rapid learning tool for the organization. It helps gain insight to the many thorny questions associated with the value realization and optimization steps of a transformation initiative. It provides the means for leaders with differing perspectives to hash out the many problems and projects associated with driving value out of an investment in people, process and technology. It provides a pictorial view of the desired benefit, Meaningful Use value lever and the work that must be done to realize value. While not a replacement for detailed project plans, problem lists and tracking tools, it provides a focal point for communication about value realization.

Creation of a Value Map facilitates many conversations and forces clarity of logic (see Figure 4-4). The ultimate customers of the Value Mapping process are the key stakeholders of the integrated system and process. The Value Map often makes a great cover sheet for more detailed

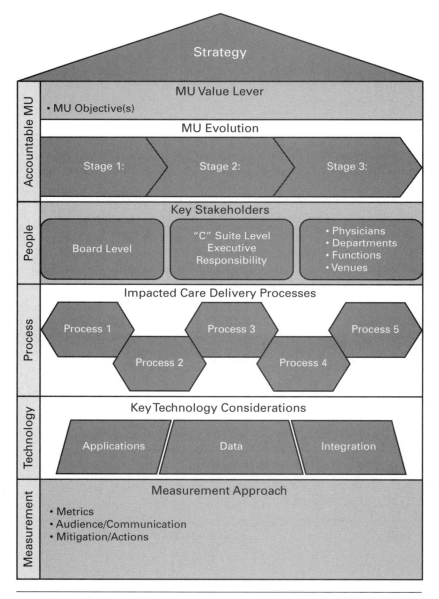

FIGURE 4-4: Sample Meaningful Use Value Map.

business cases, communication plans, risk and problem lists, etc. The key components of the Value Map are discussed in more detail in Chapters 4, 5 and 6. They include:

- **Strategy:** What is the enterprise or community health strategy that most closely aligns with the Meaningful Use initiative?
- **Meaningful Use Lever:** This is the specific Meaningful Use objective whose attainment will allow the stated strategy to be achieved. In order to meet that Meaningful Use objective, it is important to review the history and purpose of that specific Meaningful Use criterion. Reviewing the proposed and final rule will provide insight into why the objective was developed and the desired outcome/value to be achieved. In addition, it is critical to know what is expected to evolve over time as progression is made from Stage 1 to Stages 2 and 3. Finally, it is important to understand how the activity has functioned pre-automation (in a paper-based world), and how the EHR can or should change how it is applied.
- **People:** It is critical to identify both direct and indirect key stakeholders—those within the organization, as well as in the broader community. Stakeholders will be present at various levels of multiple organizations and understanding the political agendas for each will impact decisions and actions. Engagement at the top level (enterprise boards and community leadership) is essential for communicating the desire and intent to not only meet the Meaningful Use objective, but to manage value throughout the effort. Accountability must be assigned at the senior leadership level to assure that the appropriate resources are being designated to carry out the steps necessary to accomplish the goals. Achieving Meaningful Use will also require assembling a multi-disciplinary team to design new workflows and implement the technology—this will include clinicians, informaticists and IT.
- **Process:** Identification of the care delivery process that will be affected in deploying each Meaningful Use objective must occur, with awareness of the upstream and downstream effects of workflow changes. Key participants in the care delivery process, including physicians, must be involved to re-design processes that meet the Meaningful Use objectives and produce greater value. Integration of best practices from other organizations, as well as awareness of potential unintended consequences will be required. Finally, a critical success factor in deploying value-based processes will be education and training around re-designed processes and workflows.

- **Technology:** Consideration should be given to the specific IT application, as well as infrastructure, standards, integration tools, etc. The value map should include the necessary infrastructure to support the software: is there enough data storage; is there enough "bandwidth" to support access into the EHR for the anticipated number of users; what will system response time be? Consideration must also be given to the data included in the EHR and any associated data repositories—including what form the data will take, how we can create structured data where free text or scanned images were used before and what standardized vocabularies will be used (ICD-9/10, CPT, SNOMED, LOINC, RxNORM, etc.). It is also critical to document your plan for integration: how will information flow across applications within the organization, as well to other stakeholders outside the enterprise, and what interfaces or other communications platforms will need to be built? Finally, attention should be given to how the validity of the data will be monitored, along with action plans to detect and address data deficiencies: who will check, how often, what will be checked and what remediation plans must be developed to ensure that complete and valid information is stored in the EHR.

- **Measurement:** While it is important to be able to measure whether an objective is being met or not, the broader question of "how will we know we are achieving value?" should also be built into your measurement plan. Key questions you should plan to answer in your value map include: "What metrics will we use?" This may be more than the mere numerator and denominator as specified in the rule, but trending over time, or achievement at the individual provider level. It may be appropriate to set internal targets (whether based on industry benchmarks or internal performance goals). You must also identify the audiences that will be informed of results and the frequency with which results will be shared. Finally, your measurement plan should include how results will be acted upon to ensure continuous improvement, especially as the organization progresses through the various stages of Accountable Meaningful Use.

The Value Map does not relieve leaders of the need to make hard decisions, but it does quickly illustrate accountability for those decisions. Rather than assuming health IT and the CIO have responsibility for Meaningful Use compliance, it clearly demonstrates who the key stakeholders are and points to where accountability should rest. Development and execution of the Value Map is where the benefit of the technology is derived; therefore, it needs to be produced in consultation with key stakeholders. Specific steps toward its development include:

- Develop a "straw-man" Value Map for validation with key stakeholders.
- During targeted sessions (e.g. hour-long workshops), obtain agreement with the stakeholders who have knowledge of the strategies, best practices, Meaningful Use levers, assumptions, barriers, etc., to ensure:
  - All the stakeholders understand the scope and desired outcome.
  - All the risks/assumptions are out in the open.
  - Accountability is assigned and status reporting structure is clear.
  - All aspects of people, process and technology have been identified.
  - Key measures are identified.

Eleven example Value Maps are depicted in the following pages with corresponding text explaining their development and use.

Strategy: *Cost Reduction*

Lori Bishop

Introduction

Healthcare costs are consuming over 17 percent of the U.S. gross domestic product (GDP) and growing at a rate that exceeds inflation.[35] According to the Congressional Budget Office, rising healthcare costs are the biggest challenge of U.S. fiscal policy—"no other single factor will exert more influence over the long-term balance of the federal budget."[36] It is no surprise, therefore, that the U.S. healthcare system is receiving great attention and challenge from both the public and private sectors of the economy.

Understanding the drivers of the increased costs is critical to creating change that will impact the trajectory of the cost curve and not simply shift costs to other segments of society. Several studies indicate that an ever-increasing aging and obese population are key drivers of cost increases.[37] While certainly these are contributing factors, according to a recent study by Roehrig & Rousseau, the biggest factor in the increased cost is not in the prevalence (i.e., increased occurrence of disease) as one might expect, but rather in the treatment cost per case.[38] If cost per case had been held constant during the ten-year period 1996–2006, healthcare spending per capita would have grown at a pace *less* than the U.S. GDP. Consequently, while prevention is important and will help, the providers of healthcare must focus on ways to treat the sick in a more cost-effective manner.

What Is the Pay-Off/Outcome?

Reducing the cost of treating an individual patient upon presenting with a disease requires information about the patient, the treatment and the outcomes. The creation of a list of patients with a selected disease is the first step in mining and analyzing data. It requires that caregivers keep problem lists updated and in structured data. When this happens several benefits accrue:

- **Narrows focus to high-cost problems:** Trying to impact the cost of delivering care is daunting. It is important to narrow the focus to specific problems that are creating the biggest costs, have the largest variation in care or least effective outcomes. In this manner, resources can be targeted to achieve the greatest benefit.

- **Captures complete list of patients in cohort:** By using the problem list to select patients in a specific cohort, the analyst can capture patients for whom a problem exists but may not be the reason for treatment. This should allow better analysis and research to understand relationships between diseases and potentially avoid costly outcomes through proactive identification of higher-risk patients.
- **Supports proper application of evidence-based medicine:** A big factor in reducing costs per case is reduction in treatment variation and application of methods that have greater likelihood for positive outcomes. The logic and data used to create the patient list will be the tool caregivers need to categorize patients into the appropriate protocol and for use in clinical decision support.

Meaningful Use Value Lever

Accurately identifying patients with a specific problem is the first step in making meaningful improvements in quality, safety and efficiency. To meet the objective of creating a list of patients with a specific condition, the eligible provider or hospital must first have an active problems list recorded in structured data. Because the problem list is broader than the specific issue related to the episode of illness, the treatment can be evaluated more holistically for a particular disease state.

Assuming the problem list is complete and recorded with structured data, patients can be proactively identified for customized treatment, easily identified for studies and research of particular patient populations and included in statistics used to evaluate quality of care. The patient list will be a key consumer of the problem list data and, as such, the two Meaningful Use criteria will need to go hand in hand.

Alignment with Transformation Strategy

Reducing the cost of medical care is one of the key aims of Meaningful Use (see Figure 4-5). While the focus from a policy perspective is on the macro level of population health, a more micro look at cost per case is equally important and even more so for individual organizations. The payments for Medicare and Medicaid patients within an inpatient setting are already on a prospective basis by encounter; however, regulation and modifications are continuously moving closer to a payment per

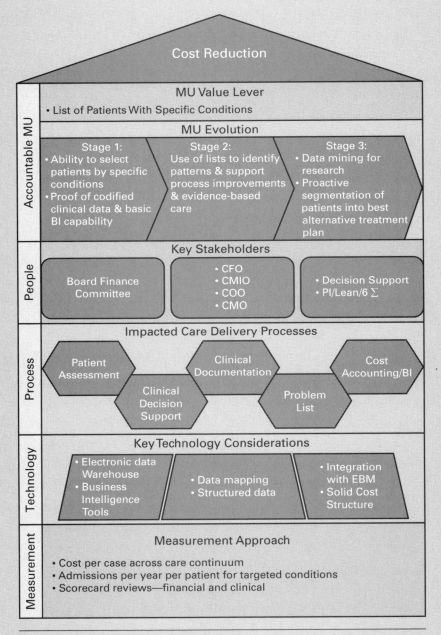

FIGURE 4-5: Cost Reduction Value Map.

case across the continuum of care. This is still episodic in nature rather than population- or panel-based; therefore, understanding how to be efficient and effective with the treatment once intervention is required is very important to all of the providers who are part of the treatment protocol.

Organizations that create the capability to use data that previously went relatively unexamined will be the ones that have a better chance of providing the value sought by the patients. Looking at cost information from a holistic patient perspective and then being able to utilize that information to effectively address similar problems in the future is key to meaningfully impacting the cost and quality of treatment.

Accountability

Achieving a reduction in cost per case and making a meaningful impact on cost of medical care will require strong leadership and accountability by both clinical leaders and the chief financial officer (CFO) of the organization. Working with clinical leaders, CFOs must ensure the organization understands how care decisions impact the value patients are receiving and can make appropriate trade-offs as the patient flows through the care-continuum.

Processes that Will Impact Realizing this Benefit

The ability to reduce cost by focusing improvement efforts on patients with a specific condition will impact up-front processes involving documentation and assessment, as well as back-end processes involving quality reporting and business analysis. Specifically,

1. **Patient Assessment:** Getting a patient on the right protocol early in the process is very important to reducing the cost per case. Since a case is made up of a series of encounters over various sites of care, the initial assessment upon presentation must include review of current problem lists, diagnostic results and previous discharge summaries available through information exchanges, patient-supplied medical records from other providers or historical patient medical records within a facility. Based upon the information from these sources, patients can then be appropriately assessed and treated early in their encounter, and hopefully, the speed and effectiveness of the care will be improved.
2. **Clinical Documentation and Problem Lists:** Having complete data in a structured format is critical to identifying patients. The process of documenting diseases and keeping a problem list current and relevant will need to be critically examined and standardized. For instance, providers must have common understanding of who owns the problem list, what will be included and how it will be structured.

Without a good documentation and problem list process, the patient lists could potentially be incomplete, excluding patients from key treatments, underestimating the denominator for quality reporting and inaccurately analyzing outcomes for process improvement and cost reductions.

3. **Cost Accounting:** Identifying high cost and low-quality patient cohorts is the first step in understanding where to apply business intelligence and process improvement resources. However, it is equally important to be able to accurately assess the true cost of treating that cohort. Many cost accounting systems fall short of this goal in two ways: costs are based upon averages rather than on actual resources consumed by case (i.e., standard cost v. job cost), and cost per case is generally limited to an episode rather than longitudinally over time. Both of these factors will need to be addressed in redesigned, repositioned cost-accounting systems if the promise of reduced cost per case is to be realized. Only then can variability in cost and care patterns be addressed to demonstrate value.

Best Practice

Best practice will evolve as the data get richer and more standardized. Getting the benefit of structured data initially will result from the ability to identify and focus cost, quality and efficiency improvement programs on those patient groups causing the biggest variances. Over time, the best practices should ultimately transition from retrospective to prospective use of the information:

- Retrospective categorization of patients with problems that result in high cost of treatment and/or poor quality outcomes for use in process improvement programs.
- Proactive identification of patients for application of evidence-based treatments and for use in clinical decision support.
- Prospective selection of patient cohorts for research and outreach for preventative measures that will ultimately reduce cost per case.

Conclusion

Value comes when data are turned into information that is meaningful and actionable. The possibilities for healthcare organizations to use the data that will be created from the efforts of the HITECH legislation are vast. The ability to understand what is causing the increased costs or ineffective outcomes for specific disease states will be greatly improved when information is organized and structured in a meaningful way. Once this knowledge is gained, processes and treatments can be put into place that will help achieve the real aims of Meaningful Use: to improve the quality and affordability of medical care.

Keys to Success:
1. Accurate, structured problem lists
2. Robust business intelligence tools and analysis
3. Effective process improvement programs

Strategy: *Clinical Quality*

Susan Irby

Introduction

Measurement of clinical quality has evolved over time in both the acute and ambulatory settings. While there are many organizations that stress improving clinical quality such as the Leapfrog Group and the Institute for Health Improvement, the importance of quality garnered national attention with the Institute of Medicine's landmark publication in 1999, "To Err is Human: Building a Safer Healthcare System."[39] There are numerous organizations and government entities that require measurement and reporting of quality for reimbursement (CMS) and as part of their certification process (The Joint Commission and others). Many organizations also participate in benchmarking collaboratives where quality is a key component of overall performance management. The "state" of quality measurement today is one where there are 744 different measures catalogued and specified by the National Quality Forum (NQF). These range from prevention and risk mitigation to screening, diagnosis and treatment.

As healthcare reform continues and reimbursement methods continue to evolve, the ability to demonstrate patient-centric quality care will be essential for organizations to survive. As a result, organizations must move from a hospital-centric inpatient focus on quality as a single episode to a healthcare community collaborative effort across venues of care.

What Is the Pay-Off/Outcome?

Clinical Quality Improvements will result in reduced costs for the healthcare delivery system as a whole as the numbers of acute episodes are reduced and care for chronic conditions can be managed in an ambulatory versus an acute setting. Here are three examples of quality metrics that must be reported in Stage 1 and how they have value to the patient and to the healthcare delivery system:

- **Flu shot for at-risk populations:** As a preventative measure, by ensuring a greater proportion of the population receives preventive care, the incidence of disease will be reduced, and the number of patients who need treatment in both the ambulatory and acute setting will be significantly reduced.

- **Emergency department throughput:** By reducing the time from decision to admit to time departed the unit and moved to an inpatient unit, initiation of treatment can begin more quickly, reducing not only the total length of stay (and associated cost of care) but improving outcomes with reduced complications associated with delay of treatment.
- **Anticoagulant drugs at discharge for stroke patients:** Using pharmacotherapy as part of the aftercare plan for patients when they are discharged from the acute care setting helps to reduce the risk of recurrence of stroke and subsequent readmission, as well as the risk for additional morbidities/mortalities.

Meaningful Use Value Lever

Improvement of Clinical Quality (see Figure 4-6) is one of the keys to Meaningful Use's first pillar, which is to "Improve quality, safety, efficiency, and reduce health disparities."[40] The impact of "doing things right the first time," as embraced by manufacturing industries and of late by service industries, is now becoming the mandate in healthcare where the consequences of poor quality are reflected in mortality and morbidity rates. By developing an enterprise approach to clinical quality monitoring and continuous improvement, organizations position themselves not only to meet this national agenda but to impact the quality of care and outcomes for the population they serve.

Alignment with Transformation Strategy

Most healthcare organizations have as part of their mission, vision and values the imperative to deliver high-quality care for their patients. In addition, those who state they wish to be the "provider of choice" must ensure that the delivery of high-quality care can be documented for the patient population they serve. However, this is not enough. Organizations must expand their quality efforts to include:

- **Establishment of a Clinical Quality Improvement and Measurement Strategy**—This includes creating a reporting relationship to a Quality Committee of the Board.[41] Current trends indicate that boards will devote more of their meeting time to discussing quality than to discussing financial performance.

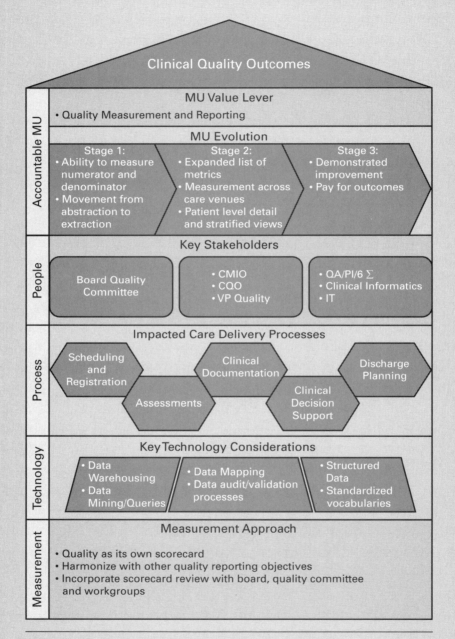

FIGURE 4-6: Clinical Quality Outcomes Value Map.

- **Positioning for Value-based Reimbursement and Participation in (or spearheading of) Accountable Care Organization and Integrated Clinical Model**—By measuring, reporting and improving on quality-based metrics, organizations can demonstrate that they are delivering outcomes that merit best reimbursement.

Accountability

Ideally, the responsibility for achieving quality clinical outcomes rests with the Chief Clinical Quality Officer (CCQO) or Vice President of Quality within the organization. For organizations where that position does not exist, the accountability cannot rest at a departmental level but must be elevated to the Chief Executive Officer (CEO) or Chief Operating Officer (COO) to receive the level of attention that will be necessary as reimbursement models shift to pay for quality outcomes.

Processes that Will Impact Clinical Quality

1. **Scheduling and Registration:** Collection of key demographic information will enable stratification of data along sex, age and racial cohorts. In addition, information such as advanced directives will allow those analyzing patient data with respect to quality metrics to identify patients to be included and excluded for each metric.
2. **Clinical Assessments:** Obtaining the patient's history and physical examination, as well as the nursing assessment and inputs from other clinicians is not enough. Identification of primary and secondary diagnoses, as well as any co-morbidities, must be entered in the patient record as structured data (problem list) using standardized terminology (ICD9/10, SNOMED) that can later be used to identify select groups of patients for study.
3. **Clinical Documentation:** As care is delivered, information about that care must also appear as structured data. This includes lab tests and associated values (LOINC), medications administered (RxNorm) and procedures performed (ICD 9/10, CPT).
4. **Clinical Decision Support:** Utilization of the rules engine associated with clinical decision support systems provides an excellent way to build quality into the clinical workflow. By programming in rules such as anti-thrombolytic drugs at a certain point in a patient's

stay, the organization can ensure that quality-driven evidence based medicine and best practices are made available for their patients.

5. **Discharge Planning/Care Coordination:** Since many factors impacting outcomes and quality of care are associated with transitions of care, planning the necessary next steps for a patient at discharge is critical. With chronic conditions, it is essential to coordinate with the primary care physician and work within the patient's medical home to monitor key indicators of managing the disease state. For all patients, follow-up visits, therapies and discharge medications all will affect the ultimate outcome for the episode.

Best Practice

Best practice will continue to evolve as organizations begin to attest for Stage 1 and move to Stage 2 and as a community of care collaborates across care venues. Here are some of the main items that high-performing organizations are doing today:

- **Harmonization of Quality Reporting Across Quality Initiatives:** With so many different quality reporting bodies and initiatives, organizations must choose which items they will report on, the timing for each and the audience(s) for results reporting.
- **Use of Structured Data:** Leveraging the power of the EHR by using standard code sets and placing the data in specified locations in the EHR mining the data (extraction) is enabled.
- **Integration into Workflow:** Ability to automate manual process of collecting and reporting quality measures is the ultimate value lever because data are recorded as care is delivered in a format that can later be queried to produce the quality metrics that the organization is reporting.
- **Integration with Performance Improvement Initiatives:** Many organizations separate their performance improvement (PI) activities from their quality assurance (QA) activities when the Plan-Do-Check-Act (PDCA) Cycle or Lean/Six Sigma is ideally suited for the goal of continuous quality improvement.
- **Target Setting and Measurement Against Target:** Organizations should track progress on a Score Card (Quality deserves a scorecard of its own). Incorporate scorecard review with appropriate leadership and working groups.
- **Concurrent Quality Management:** The ability to identify patient populations at admission or diagnosis will facilitate management

of patients with specific conditions (e.g., congestive heart failure or diabetes) across the continuum of care, resulting in earlier, appropriate interventions to improve outcomes.

Conclusion

Value comes when quality initiatives are integrated with technology implementation to produce a vehicle for measuring, reporting and acting on results. Quality of Care will continue to improve as feedback loops are developed and incorporated into the Continuous Quality Improvement cycle across care venues. EHRs are critical to realizing clinical quality because they allow a standardized way to document patient care and a way to build quality care into the workflow through clinical decision support rules. Breakthrough opportunities are in the areas of standardizing data collection and then analyzing across care venues to identify new ways of delivering care.

Keys to Success:
1. Use of structured data to mine and report quality metrics
2. Integration of clinical decision support rules and evidence-based medicine
3. Feedback loop on performance to improve process

Strategy: *Operating Efficiency*

Kevin Martin

Introduction

Healthcare systems and healthcare operations have grown increasingly complex over the years and are just recently moving toward an electronic-based clinical information system. Most hospitals across the U.S. are in some form of a hybrid state between paper and electronic documentation, and the scale of the complexity has made the transition to an electronic platform extremely challenging, affecting all areas of healthcare operations.

However, the HITECH Act is driving a great deal of change today and perhaps the most influential and fundamental change from both cultural and operational perspective is Computerized Provider/Physician Order Entry (CPOE). Order entry is the driving mechanism for patient care in this knowledge-based service, so this fundamental shift from paper to electronic orders impacts all areas of the operations: physician order entry, nursing order receiving, unit secretary order communication, pharmacy order checking, etc. Almost every area of clinical operations is impacted, so transitioning to CPOE requires strong leadership and communication.

What Is the Pay-Off/Outcome?

The Healthcare Information and Management Systems Society (HIMSS)[42] recognizes the following major benefits with CPOE:

- **Enhanced patient safety:** Medication errors attribute to the largest cause of adverse events in a hospital, and CPOE helps to minimize this in two ways. First, CPOE reduces transcription errors between the physician, nurse, unit secretary and receiving department (pharmacy, laboratory, radiology, respiratory therapy, etc). Second, electronic order entry can trigger immediate clinical decision support mechanisms in the way of system alerts for allergies and drug/drug interaction. This must be monitored carefully with clinicians to avoid alert fatigue, rendering reminders ineffective.

- **Reduced variation in care:** By closely tying CPOE with best practices through the use of evidence-based information, providers are better able to remain up to speed on the latest research and ever-changing information in the medical field. Arming providers with current evidence at the right time will help standardize care and assist in further research in the future.
- **Reduced costs due to adverse drug events:** By reducing adverse drug events (ADEs) through the use of CPOE, many studies have found that hospital stays can be significantly reduced. Additionally, a clinician's ability to offer alternative medications or lower costs through the use of clinical decision support can assist with cost savings.
- **Increased operational efficiency:** There has been a great deal written about the inefficiency of CPOE from the provider's perspective—providers can initially be as much as 20–50 percent less productive utilizing CPOE. This can be true at the initial launch of CPOE, but it is highly dependent on the system being used and the amount of physician involvement in determining workflows before deployment. However, efficiency should be measured by the time it takes to not only communicate the order but also act upon that order. Written orders add an additional step when the physician passes the order to another person, like a unit secretary, for entry into the system. This delay can add anywhere from 15–60 minutes in the communication of the order in the system and can also add opportunities for error. This time lost is far greater than the amount of time for a physician to enter the order, but physician efficiency of order entry should always be considered a top priority for CPOE deployment.

Meaningful Use Value Lever

Operational Efficiency is strongly tied to the "Improvement of Quality, Safety, & Efficiency" pillar of the HITECH Act. Quality, safety and efficiency must be tightly woven together throughout all healthcare operations, since improvement in cost cannot adversely affect quality or safety and vice versa.

The Office of the National Coordinator (ONC) recognizes the importance of CPOE for streamlining operational efficiency across the healthcare continuum, and the Department of Health & Human Services responded in the Federal Register with the following:

> *"CPOE is a foundational element to many of the other objectives of meaningful use including exchange of information and clinical decision support. CPOE has been a major initiative of US hospitals for over a decade and is a foundational functionality to many of the activities that further the health care policy priorities of meaningful use medications the patient is taking. Another benefit of CPOE is that it greatly simplifies the workflow process of inputting information into certified EHR technology in a structured way to populate the patient record."[43]*

Alignment with Transformation Strategy

CPOE should be closely integrated with the organization's overall migration toward the use of an EHR. CPOE is the initial point in which the highest clinical decision maker in the healthcare setting enters information to trigger the treatment of a patient. Therefore, CPOE should be tightly intertwined with clinical operations including areas such as nursing documentation, physician documentation, medication reconciliation and clinical decision support (see Figure 4-7).

Recognizing that the initial implementation period will in fact make the organization less efficient as practitioners must learn a new way to document, receive and disseminate patient information, the ultimate benefit to the patient will be in the form of safer care, to the provider through improved information for treatment options and to the organization and industry in overall lower cost for better outcomes. All of these benefits will eventually outweigh the "pain" of implementation. Similarly, CPOE is much more than obtaining a certain percentage of orders entered into the clinical system as they progress through the three stages of meaningful use. It is important that CPOE be linked with four areas:

- Clinical Decision Support.
- Medication Management.
- Evidence-based Medicine.
- Physician Documentation.

Accountability

The success of CPOE lies not with the CIO or Information Technology, but with clinical leadership. For organizations with a Chief Medical Information Officer (CMIO), that person should serve as the champion

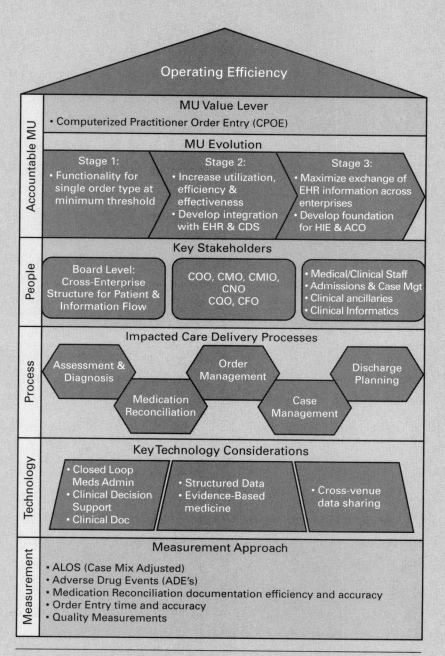

FIGURE 4-7: Operating Efficiency Value Map.

to promote adoption among providers and drive change around adoption of evidence-based medicine, standardized order sets, clinical decision support rules and approach to problem lists.

Processes that Will Impact Realizing this Benefit

1. **Medication Reconciliation:** Medication reconciliation for most organizations is a manually intensive process fraught with errors and inconsistencies at many different points throughout the patient's journey across the care continuum. The only real way to reconcile medications is through an investigative approach, extracting information from the patient and past medical encounters that may or may not be known to the clinician. Recording orders electronically provides a trail of decisions made by clinicians throughout the care processes providing the right information at the right time. When organizations have graduated from a focus on EMRs to EHRs, this benefit is then greatly increased by sharing information between enterprises, improving efficiency and accuracy for patients and clinicians alike.

2. **Order Management:** Aside from the obvious changes, the order management process itself will become more efficient over time by eliminating the wasted time handling paper orders multiple times. There should be a concerted effort in the design phase of CPOE to minimize the number of keystrokes, screen changes, unnecessary alert notifications, and overall inefficiencies for the physicians. In addition, organizations should focus on a concerted effort for 6–12 months after CPOE implementation, striving to improve physician workflow and minimize time spent behind the computer screen. Evidence-based orders will become more accurate and integrated over time as the appropriate information is provided to physicians at the right time in the right format enabling a more informed decision-making process.

3. **Assessment and Diagnosis:** Physicians will have access to previous orders and results as the EHR grows in capability, allowing them quick access to accurate information over the course of the patient's medical history. As this information is integrated with the EHR, physicians will more easily see active and discontinued orders.

4. **Case Management and Discharge:** Perhaps the most improved area from an operational perspective within the hospital will be the case management and discharge process. Many hospitals struggle to implement a seamless process supporting case managers who must

Keys to Success:
1. Make it easy, intuitive & accurate for physicians to use
2. Integrate evidence-based practice and appropriate level of clinical decision support
3. Incorporate medication reconciliation and clinical documentation

initiate dozens of phone calls and inquiries to transfer a patient from the hospital to home or another facility. With the orders recorded and resulted in electronic format, it makes the compilation of information easier for case managers, the patient and receiving facilities.

Best Practice

Best practice will continue to evolve as organizations begin to attest for Stage 1 and move to Stage 2, but lessons learned in the past decade from CPOE groundbreakers include the following:

- **Development of Usable Order Sets:** Organizations that are successful in deploying and utilizing CPOE almost always have one thing in common: very accurate, easy-to-use and easily adaptable order sets. Order sets are the backbone to the efficient use of CPOE for physicians, the beginning of standardized care, and an extremely vital part of integrating evidence-based practices. Organizations should take great care when developing order sets, and the best organizations take the time to review all order sets—they do not simply copy and paste the old written order sets. It is also paramount to decide early on how the organization will manage new information and incorporate that information into the orders; best practices show that a management structure is established to capture the information, review the information, and incorporate the information all through a very specific process.

- **Incorporating Clinical Decision Support at the Appropriate Levels:** The most common examples of clinical decision support for CPOE can be found in drug/drug and drug/allergy interactions. At one 500+ bed facility, it was found that if all potential interactions were activated, physicians and pharmacists would need to deal with more than 25,000 alerts per day. Alert fatigue has the adverse effect on the desire to use CPOE to improve quality and must be carefully monitored and reviewed by the medical staff. Metrics are put in place at high-performing facilities to monitor these interactions to optimize valuable use and eliminate overuse.

- **Deployment of Continuous Improvement Strategies Across Clinicians:** This is a hallmark of organizations that are serious about the long-term use of CPOE because there is a realization that the systems are not designed perfectly the first time. Otherwise, why would there be so much resistance to CPOE over the past ten years? The best demonstrated practice for organizations is to develop performance improvement groups that work on the front lines with clinicians to study workflow and optimize operations at the user level to enhance the sending and receiving of information.

Conclusion

Value is achieved when an organization is able to implement CPOE in a sustainable fashion and, after six months, physicians admit they prefer using CPOE over written orders. However, the real value comes when an organization realizes that CPOE is a vital step in developing a comprehensive EHR, and the effort is made to connect medication reconciliation, order management, clinical decision support and physician documentation.

> "CPOE shouldn't be seen as just a means to enter orders. If it were just that, it would be easy. It should be used as a means to revolutionize a hospital system through workflow analysis and optimization."
>
> **Asif Ahmed**
> **Chief Information Officer**
> **Duke University Health Systems**

In order to achieve this meaningful use objective, organizations must make a very concerted effort to study technology and clinical workflows impacting operations. Almost every organization will say they understand this, but the true test is to produce the accompanying changes in workflows. Organizations that are serious about this integration and realize over 50 percent of their operational costs are derived from workforce compensation, will take the time to document and study the workflows with a cross-functional team including physicians, nurses, unit secretaries, medical records, pharmacy, laboratory, radiology, pulmonary, dietary, case management and clinical informatics.

The long-term breakthrough opportunities exist when the organization is beyond the internal operational improvement of CPOE, beyond the outpatient integration of CPOE and beyond the internal IT integration of CPOE—these all support a fully integrated EHR. The long-term benefit comes with a fully functional EHR that will support information sharing across enterprises and across markets/communities. The breakthrough will come when organizations are focused on sharing this information, enabling a healthcare model that reimburses on value and not on service.

Strategy: *Provider Access and Effectiveness*

Vicki Miller

Introduction

Over the years, advances in medicine and provider specialization have increased the number of sites where care is delivered to patients. Currently, as patients move between ambulatory, acute, and post-acute care settings, new providers receive little or no information from the patient's previous providers. Often, the receiving providers rely on the patient's knowledge of the care provided or divert time from direct patient care to contacting past providers to develop the care history. Providers who do receive information often find it challenging to review the information received, generally on paper, to find the essential data quickly. The lack of summarized, timely care information during care transitions can lead to confusion about the patient's condition and appropriate care, duplicate tests, inconsistent patient monitoring, medication errors, delays in diagnosis and lack of follow through on referrals The lack of communication may contribute to patient safety, quality of care and outcome issues. Furthermore, this limitation places significant financial burden on patients and the U.S. healthcare system as a whole. All of these variables contribute to patient and family caregivers' dissatisfaction with the U.S. healthcare system.

A study of referrals by 22 pediatricians conducted in 2000 regarding specialty referrals and physician satisfaction with referrals found that no information was sent to the specialist in 49 percent of the referrals, while the referring physician received feedback from the specialist only 55 percent of the time.[44] These numbers have not increased materially since this earlier study. Patients with chronic conditions, expected to reach 157 million in the U.S. by 2020, may visit up to sixteen physicians in a year.[45] Providing a succinct summary of care received at each transition is an important aspect of increasing providers' access and effectiveness when delivering care (see Figure 4-8). New technologies will

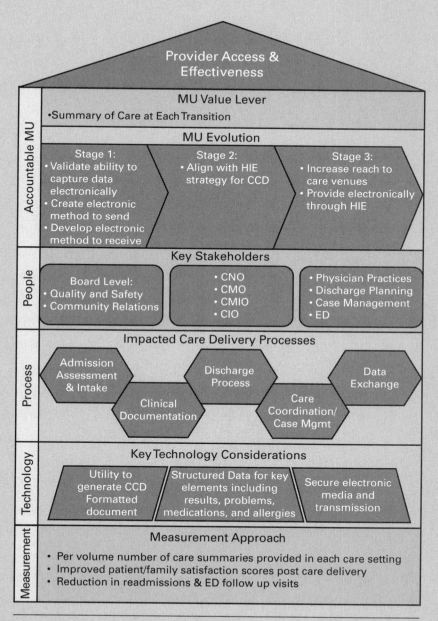

FIGURE 4-8: Provider Access & Effectiveness Value Map.

enable access to care summaries electronically, potentially eliminating today's manual processes, allowing providers to work more effectively and improve the quality and effectiveness of care delivery.

What Is the Pay-Off/Outcome?

The National Transitions of Care Coalition (NTOCC) defines a transition of care as the movement of patients between healthcare locations, providers, or different levels of care within the same location as their conditions and care needs change.[46] Timely, accurate and effective communication between caregivers, patients, and their families during the transition of care is an expected capability of meaningfully-used, interoperable EHRs. When effectively implemented, potential benefits include:

- **Improved Provider Workflow:** The need to search through extensive medical records or contact other caregivers for information regarding prior care is reduced and potentially eliminated with the exchange of the summary of care.
- **Reduction in Readmission:** With an understanding of the care previously given, the new provider can maintain treatment continuity, potentially reducing the need for visits to emergency departments or readmission as a result of a miscommunication on follow-up care expectations.
- **Risk Reduction:** Information about a patient's current medications, treatments and problems provided at the care transition to future care providers has the potential to reduce patient risk.
- **Reduction in Duplicate Tests & Procedures:** Availability of tests and procedures and related results eliminates the need to repeat tests unnecessarily because information was not available at the time of treatment by the new provider.
- **Improved Patient & Family Engagement in Care:** The written, concise summary of care, whether in the acute or ambulatory setting, provides a better communication tool regarding care provided, medications, and results, potentially eliminating the need to contact care providers for follow up information.

Meaningful Use Value Lever

Providing a summary of care at each transition point is a key to the HITECH goal to "Improve Care Coordination." To meet the objective, an organization (eligible hospital or critical access hospital) that transitions a patient to another setting or provider of care or refers the patient to another provider of care should provide a summary of care record (Continuity of Care Document) for each transition for 50 percent or more of the transitions of care and referrals.

The summary of care can be provided via electronic exchange (e.g., directly between the provider's EHRs) or on paper, provided the paper is generated by the transitioning provider's EHR. When a paper process is used, the patient must be able and reasonably expected to deliver the document to the next provider. At a minimum, based on the Meaningful Use guidelines, the summary of care record should include diagnostic tests results, problem list, medication list and medication allergy list. Organizations should consider including other information, such as the plan of care that will support the goals of improving provider access and efficiency.

Alignment with Transformation Strategy

As organizations prepare for changes in the way healthcare is delivered and reimbursed, planning the effective and efficient communication between care transitions is vital. Introduction of value-based purchasing, combined payment structures and expanded quality reporting under healthcare reform all require an organization to think beyond the traditional hospital or ambulatory service to manage care quality and cost.

In a September 2010 report, the NTOCC outlined in its vision for improving care transitions seven areas of consideration for organizations seeking to improve transitions of care.[47] Among the seven is "Improve communication during transitions between providers, patients, and family caregivers." NTOCC offers further guidance on improving the communication as patients move between care settings, including:

- Provide patients and family caregivers the tools and resources to support navigation of the transition and to be "informed consumers" of care.
- Work with providers to help them communicate better during the transition of care.
- Develop standardized and universal protocols for transition from the emergency department to outpatient care.

Organizations that can seamlessly transition patients across settings and providers will be in the best position to succeed as the industry transforms.

Accountability

Clinicians must take the lead role in assuring access and effectiveness around care communications. The Chief Medical Officer (CMO), in concert with the Chief Medical Informatics Officer (CMIO) must ensure that the content of the summaries of care, as well as the means by which the summaries are communicated, are a meaningful vehicle for communicating patient information between providers.

Processes that Will Impact Realizing this Benefit

Providing a summary of care for each transition impacts processes related to patient care planning, documentation and information exchange. These processes include:

1. **Admission Assessment and Intake:** When a patient transitions to the care of a new provider, the intake process should include determining if a summary of care document is available. If available, the admission assessment process should incorporate steps to review the summary of care document, validate the information with the patient and/or family and incorporate it into the care plan.

2. **Discharge Planning:** The discharge process should include steps to ensure that the summary of care is developed and provided to the patient and the PCP. Initially for most organizations, the method of "transporting" the care summary will vary based on the receiving provider's capabilities for electronic exchange. Information must be available to discharge planning teams regarding the method of providing a summary and the actions to take (e.g., create an electronic summary, provide the patient with a paper document).

3. **Care Coordination/Case Management:** As care coordination and case management activities move beyond the acute care setting, review of the care summary should be incorporated into processes. Examples of steps to incorporate include reviewing the care summary with patients and families and validating that the providers to whom patients are referred received the care summary.

4. **Clinical Documentation:** The requirement to electronically generate the care summary from EHRs requires that data are entered in a consistent location and structured format. Organizations will need to define the content standards and ensure those documenting information follow the standards set. Determining clinical documentation standards will need to incorporate requirements beyond the organization's EHR to ensure data can be exchanged between providers both across the enterprise and in the referral network.

5. **Data Exchange:** Today's processes for exchanging information between providers are generally data-centered and performed by extracting a row or record of data in pre-determined lengths and formats (e.g., X12, Health Level 7 [HL7]) that are sent through clinical messages to a receiving system. Data exchanged becomes part of a

> **Keys to Success:**
> 1. Concise, easy to read format
> 2. Timely electronic exchange of information
> 3. Integration with care giver workflow

larger file, often without a structured approach to review the new data in context of the care delivered. To support the use of transitional care summaries, data exchange will need to become document-centered with information provided in a prearranged, structured textual format (e.g., CCD) requiring organizations to ensure data are available in the right format with the right data elements to generate the document-centric exchange.

Best Practice

Best practice will continue to evolve as organizations implement EHRs and participate in HIEs.

Organizations that are successfully realizing the value from providing transitional summaries of care will implement the following best practices:

- Develop methods and processes to ensure data are captured electronically in a structured, consistent method across all caregivers.
- Establish electronic processes to send, receive and use data provided in the transitional care summary.
- Leverage HIEs to share data between EHRs and patient portals, eliminating the need to provide data through other transportation means (e.g., the patient/family).

Conclusion

Providing care summaries at each point of transition will improve patient care by providing caregivers access to concise, timely information not readily available in the past to receiving providers. When implemented effectively, providers and their staff should realize less time spent piecing together previous care information and more time providing direct, focused patient care. Patients also benefit from this improvement through reduction in redundant testing and more consistent care as they navigate through an acute episode and/or manage ongoing chronic diseases.

Strategy: *Patient Safety*

Marla Crockett

Introduction

The need for an accurate listing of the medications a patient is currently taking has long been recognized as a way to improve patient safety and the quality of care. According to the Institute of Medicine (IOM), the average hospitalized patient is subject to at least one medication error per day. The IOM estimates that medical errors cause between 44,000 and 98,000 deaths annually in the United States. Using the more conservative figure, medical errors rank as the eighth leading cause of death, killing more Americans than motor vehicle accidents, breast cancer or AIDS (acquired immune deficiency syndrome). In addition to this extraordinary human toll, medical errors result in annual costs of $17 to $29 billion in the United States.[48] More than 40 percent of mediation errors are believed to result from inadequate reconciliation in handoffs during admission, transfer and discharge of patients.[49,50]

According to The Joint Commission, medication reconciliation is the process of comparing a patient's medication orders to all of the medications that the patient has been taking. This reconciliation is done to avoid medication errors such as omissions, duplications, dosing errors or drug interactions. It should be done at every transition of

Medication Error Potential Harm

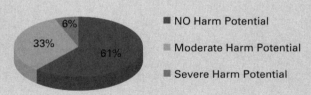

care in which new medications are ordered, or existing orders are rewritten.[51]

The HITECH act definition of medication reconciliation is focused on the transitions or handoffs in care across organizations or types of care delivery settings and does not focus on transitions of care or handoffs within a care setting. "Transition of care" is defined as the movement of a patient from one setting of care (hospital, ambulatory primary care practice, ambulatory specialty care practice, long-term care, home health, rehabilitation facility) to another. The rule also further specifies that the receiving eligible hospital (EH) or eligible provider (EP) would be responsible for conducting the medication reconciliation.[52] In both instances, the primary goal of the medication reconciliation process is to improve the safety and efficacy of patient care (see Figure 4-9).

What Is the Pay-Off/Outcome?

An effective, comprehensive medication reconciliation process should result in fewer medication errors at the point of transition of care, fewer "potential" errors and better outcomes for patients, regardless of site of delivery of care. In a 2005 study by United States Pharmacopeia (USP), the most frequent causes of reconciliation failures were as follows (multiple causes can be attributed to an event): performance deficit (88%), transcription inaccurate/omitted (84%), documentation (83%), communication (82%) and workflow disruption (80%). The analysis found that about two-thirds of the errors occurred during a patient's transition to another level of care; over one-half of the errors were intercepted before reaching the patient, and errors made upon admission were most likely to result in patient harm, including death.[53] While IT solutions are being widely studied and do appear to significantly reduce medication discrepancies, their effect on clinical outcomes remains unclear.[54]

- In any given week, 4 out of 5 adults will take a medication; 1 out of 3 will take at least 5 medications.
- One study concluded that at least 1.5 million preventable Adverse Drug Events (ADEs) occur annually in the United States.
- Each medication error can add $8,750 to the patient stay, not to mention the pain, suffering and loss of life.[55]

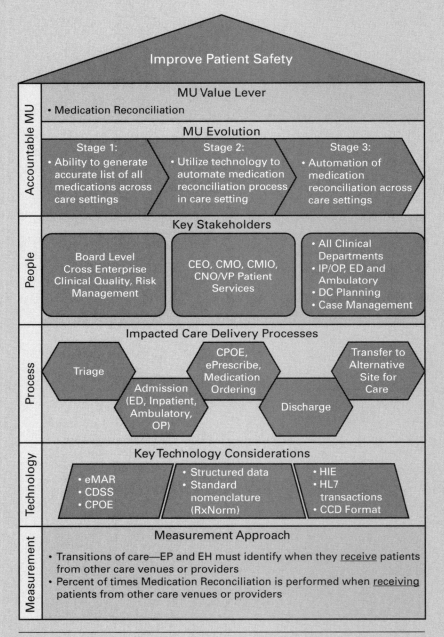

FIGURE 4-9: Improve Patient Safety Value Map.

Meaningful Use Value Lever

Medication reconciliation is directly tied to the "Improvement of Quality, Safety, & Efficiency" pillar of the HITECH Act. Quality, safety and efficiency are tightly woven together throughout all healthcare delivery, as high quality and safety lead to less rework and remediation, and thus, result in improved efficiency. When all three elements are in place, cost of care delivery can be effectively managed.

The ONC recognizes the importance of medication reconciliation across the healthcare continuum and the Department of Health & Human Services responded in the Federal Register with the following:[56]

"We certainly look forward to a time when most medication reconciliation occurs as an automated process within the EHR reconciling information that has been exchanged. However, it is unlikely that an automated process within the EHR will fully supplant the medication reconciliation conducted between the provider and the patient. In order for this automated reconciliation process to occur and be useful, the relevant structured data exchanged needs to be as accurate as possible. Requiring medication reconciliation as part of Meaningful Use in Stage 1 lays the groundwork for future reliable electronic exchange."

Alignment with Transformation Strategy

Medication reconciliation ties directly with any strategy related to patient safety and quality care. The ability to provide safe, efficient, effective care from the point at which the patient enters the health enterprise is reliant upon the accuracy and completeness of information about that patient. Understanding the patient's actual medication regimen is a large component of that important information. Because the entry into the enterprise system can be at any point of care, from the emergency department to the physician's office to the outpatient center, each point of care should initiate the medication reconciliation process.

The direct and indirect "costs" of medication errors also must be considered when organizations evaluate the fiscal responsibility pillar of their strategies. Improving patient safety by focusing on reduction in ADEs most assuredly will provide financial payback through reduced rework and remediation in addition to improved patient care.

Accountability

Medication reconciliation rests on the shoulders of multiple caregivers; within an acute care organization, physicians, nurses and pharmacists must all work together to ensure that the correct medications are documented when a patient enters and leaves the facility. The leadership responsibility for this initiative lies primarily with the Chief Nursing Officer (CNO), collaborating with the Chief Medical Officer (CMO), to coordinate activities between nurses and physicians. On the ambulatory side, the challenge is the multiple transitions not only to and from acute care but between primary care and specialists. A practice leader (Medical Director) should lead the medication Reconciliation effort.

Processes that Will Impact Realizing this Benefit

Due to the difficulty of obtaining accurate information about the patient's actual medication usage and allergies, all processes involving transition of care and adding or modifying medications will be impacted.

1. **Triage (Emergency Center or Urgent Care):** The triage process is the first point during an emergent or urgent care visit where the medication reconciliation process is initiated by a clinically trained professional. It is critical that the patient triage interview includes creating an initial list of the medications the patient is currently taking, which will be verified in greater detail with the more comprehensive admission or intake admission assessment. The triage interview process completed by a qualified clinical team member includes rapidly understanding current medications, last dose taken, route, dosage and frequency. Triage is the process of determining the priority of patients' treatments based on the severity of their condition and does not replace the more comprehensive intake interview/admission assessment.

2. **Admission (Intake):** The admission or intake process is the first point at which the medication reconciliation process is initiated after a "break in services" or when a patient first seeks care from an enterprise provider. It is critical that the patient interview includes creating a comprehensive list of the medications the patient is currently taking. Understanding that patients and/or families are not accurate or complete sources of verifiable data, the intake/interview process completed by a qualified clinical team member should include seeking verification of the patient- and/or family-reported medications

from other sources such as: old medical records, physician office medication lists, retail pharmacy data (either available via phone or through direct, electronic connections), insurance claims data and other sources.

3. **Medication Ordering (CPOE, ePrescribe and writing a prescription):** The safe process of ordering a medication for a patient to treat a specific symptom or diagnosis requires that the ordering physician or advanced practice nurse has knowledge of the current medications the patient is taking. Without current, correct knowledge of what medications the patient is taking (scheduled and as needed), the ordering practitioner puts the patient's well-being at risk through potential mediation duplications, drug/drug interactions, overdosing and other significant complications. The pharmacist plays an important role in the order completion/medication distribution sub-process for medication ordering and also provides significant input into the medication reconciliation process.

4. **Discharge (Release from Care Episode):** Discharge from an episode of care, from the care of a specific provider or site of care represents another opportunity to reconcile the medications for the patient. This step in the process is inherently more complex, as it should include not only reconciliation between what the patient has been taking while receiving care and the "discharge" medications but also a reconciliation with the medications the patient was taking before the current episode required new medications or changes in medications. It is critical that the patient (and the family) understands what medications should continue, what medications should stop and their role as a patient in reconciliation of medications with their PCP.

Keys to Success:
1. Standardize each process and sub-process
2. The process should be patient-centered
3. Limit the number of individuals involved in each step of the reconciliation process
4. Use all sources of medications history available
5. Reconcile at each transition of care as defined by ONC and The Joint Commission
6. Focus on the long-term goal of automation of the entire reconciliation process

5. **Transfer to Alternative Site or Provider of Care:** Each transfer or transition of care to an alternative provider or location requires medication reconciliation be completed and documented by the receiving party. The receiving party or location will use the reconciliation information to make future care and medication decisions for the patient.

Best Practice

Best practice will continue to evolve as organizations begin to attest for Stage 1 and move to Stage 2.

- A robust medication reconciliation process should include participation by physicians, nurses, pharmacists and patients/families.
- The process for medication reconciliation must be clearly defined by a multi-disciplinary team and responsibilities for each component of the process assigned to the parties involved.
- The process is patient-centered.
- During the discharge process, medical staff should ensure that patients are educated about any changes in medication regimen.[57]

Conclusion

Patient safety can be materially improved by reducing medication errors. Value comes when patients consistently receive the right medication, the right dose, with the right route and the right frequency. In order to meet this objective, organizations must clearly make medication safety a priority, establish zero tolerance for error, and include physicians, nurses, pharmacists and patient/family in the process. Real breakthrough opportunities will be achieved when interoperable technology combined with process standardization and role clarification becomes the norm for all caregivers in the continuum.

> "Most errors are system-based, not due to reckless individuals"
>
> **IOM: To Err is Human; 1999**[39]

Strategy: *Patient Engagement*

Bryant Hoyal

Introduction

One of the five overarching goals outlined in the HITECH Act is to engage patients and their families. As patients and their families evolve from being passive observers to active players in managing their own care, healthcare organizations must develop strategies to support and encourage this engagement. In today's environment, a patient's health information is often stored in various disparate locations. Patients, especially those with chronic conditions, must assimilate information from multiple providers. It is not uncommon for patients to receive little information about their medical condition, treatment plan, contributing factors and self-care activities. These patients are more likely to incur increased cost and experience adverse clinical outcomes.

Providing timely access to health information is an important stepping stone to engaging patients and their families (see Figure 4-10). Patients who are informed about their health status and treatment plans can play a more active role in managing their health outcomes. Patients who are confident in their understanding of their condition are often more prepared to take charge of their health and make better decisions. Informed patients who openly communicate with their physician are likely to experience fewer healthcare crises and declines in functional status. Healthcare leaders believe that patient education, active participation, self-management and a focus on prevention are the key elements for effectively managing the rise of chronic conditions as the country's population ages.[58]

These patient engagement concepts have been building blocks in developing initiatives such as patient-centered care, medical homes, Meaningful Use and accountable care. The market has responded by developing

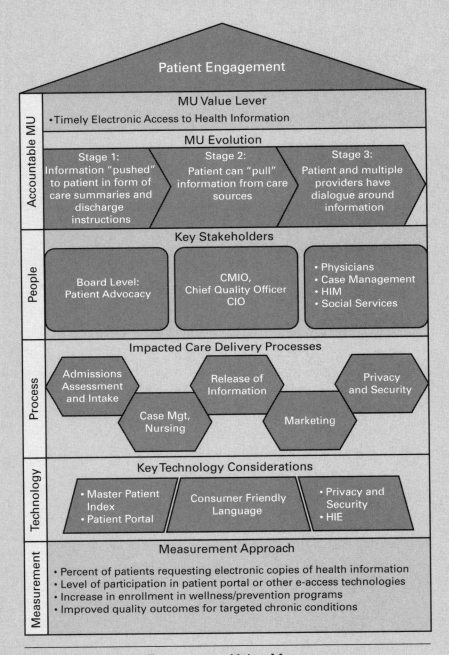

FIGURE 4-10: Patient Engagement Value Map.

IT tools to support patient-engagement activities. These tools have the power to provide substantial benefits for providers, patients and their stakeholders as a part of their patient engagement strategy.

What Is the Pay-Off/Outcome?

Providing patients with timely electronic access to their health information builds the foundation for an engaging and collaborative patient-provider relationship and results in several additional benefits including:

- **Improved Patient Outcomes:** Studies show that increases in patient engagement are associated with improvements in health-related behaviors.[59] Patient portals are a common mechanism for providing timely access to health information and facilitating patient engagement. Patients who truly understand their diagnosis, the contributing factors of their condition, and the lifestyle choices that can affect it are more likely to make positive behavioral decisions that impact their health. In addition, patients who are engaged and informed tend to communicate better with their providers and feel their relationship is more of collaborative partnership with equal responsibility and accountability leading to better decisions around treatment options and improved clinical outcomes.

- **Reduction in Cost from Lower Utilization of Services:** Patients who have access to information tend to more actively manage their chronic conditions and be aware of activities that lead to exacerbations. They are less likely to use high-cost emergency healthcare services and other resources. For example, informed asthmatic patients, who are aware of environmental triggers and proactively manage their allergy and asthma medications, are less likely to require an emergency department visit for an asthma attack. Similarly, diabetic patients who monitor their diet, exercise, medications and glucose levels using a web-based tracking system to keep their diabetes controlled are less likely to need costly eye, foot and wound care.

- **Reduction in Cost from More Informed Decision Making:** Patient engagement can also lead to cost reductions that occur when patients are informed about the medical condition and are able to make better decisions about treatment plans. There is growing belief that patients who have a full understanding of their treatment options, along with the tradeoff of risks and benefits, tend to choose more conservative, less invasive and less costly procedures.

- **Reduction in Administrative Costs:** Using technology to automate patient communication can reduce administrative costs as well. Advanced provider organizations use Internet or mobile technologies to gather patient information directly from the source such as demographic data, medical history, insurance information, and even eSignatures on waivers and forms. These practices have the potential to use fewer labor resources and may result in more accurate responses.[60]

- **Reduction in Unnecessary Readmissions:** An AARP (formerly American Association of Retired Persons) study of patients over age 50 with at least one chronic condition concluded that engaged patients who were more informed about post-discharge self-care plans were less likely to experience hospital readmissions. On the other hand, "less engaged respondents had lower transition scores and were more likely to be readmitted to a facility within 30 days."[61]

- **Reduced Likelihood of Litigation:** Another benefit of building a relationship with engaged patients is that these patients are less likely to become involved in litigation in the event of a negative clinical outcome. A study involving Bariatric Surgery patients concluded that "a good relationship with the patient and family remains the most effective way of reducing risk of being sued when there is an unfortunate complication, as well as increasing the chances of a successful defense in the event of suit."[62]

Meaningful Use Value Lever

In 2008 the National Quality Forum (NQF) released a groundbreaking document called "National Priorities and Goals."[63] The HITECH Proposed Rule states this information had a major influence on the Health IT Policy Committee as they worked to develop the objectives for achieving Meaningful Use. The NQF included patient engagement as a top priority. It says: "Patients who are active partners in their healthcare team are vital to achieving better health outcomes, lower service utilization, and lower cost."[64]

CMS clearly recognizes the relationship between access to health information and patient engagement. In the HITECH Act, CMS outlined objectives for hospitals and providers to achieve Meaningful Use of an EHR and included an objective for providing timely electronic access to health information. The objective requires, at a minimum, that 10 percent of patients should be provided access to their lab results, problem list, medication list, and allergies within four business days. Although an optional physician objective for Stage 1, this objective is expected to become a required Core objective for hospitals and providers for Stage 2. Achieving this criterion typically involves extending the data stored in the provider's EHR to the patient through an Internet-based patient portal.

CMS also outlined other objectives for patient engagement in Stage 1 including: provide patients with an electronic copy of health information and discharge instructions upon request, provide patients with clinical visit summaries and use an EHR to produce patient-specific education resources. The early projections for Stage 2 indicate that several of these objectives may be merged with the objective for providing timely electronic access to health information. Therefore, organizations should develop a strategy with a long-term focus to meet both stages and plan on the likelihood of needing to provide patients with multiple options for obtaining their information.

Alignment with Transformation Strategy

Engaging patients in their own care is foundational to improving overall health outcomes—for both the patient and the community. The benefits of patient engagement have been widely documented, potentially leading to lower costs, improved satisfaction and increased patient safety. As healthcare delivery and reimbursement models evolve, patient engagement will grow in importance as a critical success factor under these new models.

To maximize their success, organizations should develop a patient engagement strategy at the executive level. The strategy should be linked with health IT and patient and community education initiatives. Organizations should conduct systematic and thoughtful planning to define the access methods, types of information shared, timeliness of the information and additional content. A strategy for educating patients, their families and the community related to understanding and using health information is required. The patient engagement objectives should also align with the organization's strategies for care coordination, patient communication, patient-centered care and care delivery model transformation.

Accountability

Patient engagement will require leadership from executives with vision and understanding of the patient community served. The particular executive who drives this strategy will vary by organization but should be the vice president or executive in charge of patient education, patient outreach or quality. As patient engagement is so much broader than simply providing electronic access to medical records, the accountability should be aligned with patient care rather than administrative functions.

Processes that Will Impact Realizing this Benefit

Providing patient education and access to their medical information are activities that are done in healthcare organizations today; however, to truly engage patients in their own care, these activities will require modifications to several processes. Specifically,

1. **Case Management, Discharge Planning and Nursing:** Part of the patient advocacy role of case managers, discharge planners and nurses can be to educate patients on the technologies and tools available to them. The workflow for these clinicians will need to change to incorporate this information into the patient education process. The patient engagement tools can greatly reinforce information such as: condition and treatments, medications, self-care instructions after discharge, symptoms that require a follow-up visit, recommendations for monitoring and managing diet, exercise and making healthy lifestyle choices.

2. **Release of Information:** Typically, hospitals provide patients, their families and their legal representation with copies of medical records through the Release of Information service. This information has historically been delivered on paper through a time-consuming photocopying process. The Release of Information processes will need to evolve further to support the goal of timely electronic access to information. Organizations need to fully analyze the impact of adding electronic access to health information for patients. This requires evaluating the appropriate uses, updating/developing processes and procedures, determining the required authorizations for access and defining the appropriate contents electronic release. Process and procedures should include identifying patient preferences for receiving information and documenting how requests were fulfilled.

3. **Registration, Admission Assessment and Intake:** The EHR is typically initiated during the registration process. It is critical to have accurate and consistent patient identities before deploying electronic access systems. As patient health records that have historically been episodic in nature evolve to a more longitudinal focus, there is even more pressure to have clean patient identities. Organizations must work to clean master patient indexes and establish the appropriate business processes for data quality, reliability and integrity to prevent duplication and overlays. Registration processes should be reviewed and updated, as required, to minimize the requirement for "backend" review to ensure accuracy.

4. Privacy and Security: Patient engagement technologies that store, maintain or distribute electronic health information must be held to the privacy and security laws required by HIPAA and the HITECH Act. As patients and their families gain access to information electronically, security and privacy policies and procedures should be reviewed and updated. Organizations must expand their scope of risk analysis and monitoring to include the technologies used to provide electronic access.

Best Practice

Providing timely electronic access to health information for patients and families requires careful thought and analysis to determine the approach that best fits with the organization's strategy while meeting the community needs. However, most organizations find the need to expand existing technology to provide this access. The IT tools used to provide electronic access come in many forms. Regardless of the technology or approach selected, a few common trends are emerging regarding best practices:

- Incorporate education about the available tools to access health information into the clinical and administrative workflow. Clinicians should be trained on the functionality offered by these tools and should make it part of the education process to encourage their patients to access them. Likewise, revenue cycle staff should be trained on the tools and should educate patients during scheduling and registration processes.
- Prioritize privacy and security to establish a sense of trust within the patient community. Patient confidence in the security of their personal data is critical to encourage sharing of information. This basis of trust can lead to greater adoption and more successful engagement programs.
- Recognize that patient engagement is not one-size-fits-all. As a result, the technology selected must be flexible. Organizations should segment patient groups and establish specific goals for communicating with each including specific approaches, key messages and measurable outcomes.

Conclusion

One of the five pillars of the HITECH Act is engaging patients and their families in their care. The Meaningful Use requirements focus on leveraging technology to provide access to information to assist in

In a webcast launch for "Care For Your Own Care," a public-private partnership aimed at empowering patients to drive healthcare quality improvements, Director Risa Lavizzo-Mourey, MD, explained that when patients use IT to track their care, the result is better care.[65]

engaging them. Engaging patients and families with information is about more than providing electronic and timely access to information. It is also a way to foster collaborative decision making between provider and patient, improve outcomes, and reduce cost. Organizations must develop their patient engagement strategy and determine what initiatives to use to link technology and services to this strategy.

Services to inform and engage patients are popping up outside the traditional healthcare provider setting—Walgreen's Minute Clinics, Microsoft HealthVault, WebMD, Doctor Radio on Sirius XM, and the over 4,000 medical iPhone apps available. The proliferation of these services indicates that patients want information about their health and are seeking a connection with a healthcare provider. Organizations that leverage technology to communicate with and provide information to patients and their families will provide a strong foundation to meeting the goal of engaging patients and families in their own care.

Organizations can realize value from their investments in patient communication initiatives to support overall patient engagement. If managed successfully, the components of patient engagement—education, open sharing of information, collaboration and empowerment—can lead to improved health outcomes, reduced cost and increased patient loyalty.

Strategy: *Exchange of Information*

Lori Bishop

Introduction

With the statement, "By computerizing health records, we can avoid dangerous medical mistakes, reduce costs, and improve care," former president, George W. Bush in his 2004 State of the Union address began the race to use IT to slow the unimpeded growth of healthcare costs and to improve the health of U.S. citizens.[66] Since then, the health IT industry has exploded, particularly in the segments related to medical records and health information. The Office of the National Coordinator for Health Information Technology (ONC) was created and charged with developing a "health information technology infrastructure" that reduces costs and improves quality of healthcare.[67] At the center of the charge was the adoption of the electronic health record (EHR) and Health Information Exchange (HIE) systems.[68]

However, the evidence of achieving the promised benefits is difficult to see. Understandably, creators of the first generation of EHRs had much to learn about usability and acceptance by care givers. But as these barriers have slowly been overcome, the industry is still searching for the ROI. The EHR to meet all of the expectations must have interoperability with other providers in the delivery of care (see Figure 4-11). It is no longer enough to just digitize the old medical record. The caregiver must be able to see what has happened with a patient across settings and over time. This longitudinal record requires significant standardization and compliance by every caregiver in the continuum. The technology and the infrastructure to achieve this interconnection are a large part of the HITECH funding and Meaningful Use of EHRs and a core requirement for healthcare payment reform, from volume-based to value-based reimbursement.

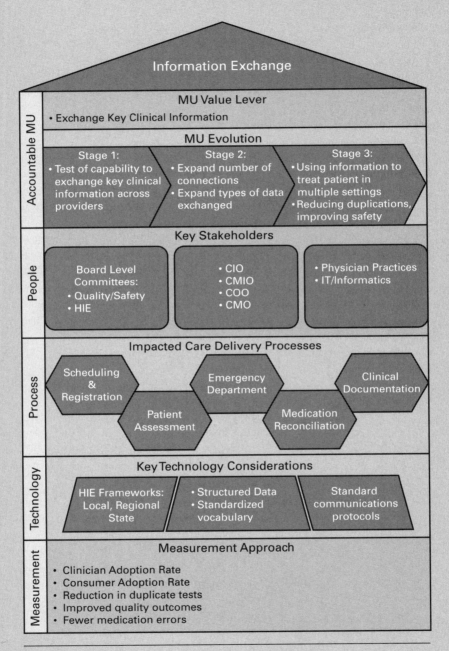

Figure 4-11: Information Exchange Value Map.

What Is the Pay-Off/Outcome?

The expected benefits from an interoperable HIE are lofty. Some are more immediate (e.g., reduction in duplicate tests) and some are longer-term, based upon the assumption that large amounts of outcomes data for a continuum of care will be available (e.g., clinical research & development of evidence-based care). These expected pay-offs include:

- **Advances in care processes:** Improved patient outcomes, improvements in safety and quality and better monitoring of diseases and other health risks.
- **Organizational benefits:** Improved organization effectiveness, as evidenced in work and quality improvement processes; communication among individuals, groups and organizations; satisfaction of needs and expectations of patients, providers and other stakeholders and organization risk mitigation.
- **Financial benefits:** Cost reduction, revenue enhancement and productivity gains.

While not every organization will achieve every benefit, all should see advances in some of these areas depending upon the specific use cases that are the foundation for the specific HIE(s) in which they participate.

Meaningful Use Value Lever

Improving care coordination is the most obvious outcome expected from HIEs. Knowing what treatments the patient has received in other settings and possibly for other problems is very important in orchestrating a cohesive treatment plan. However, less lofty functionality of HIEs such as electronic delivery of test results and interfaces with pharmacies has proven to add significant benefits in efficiency, quality and even safety of care. Anecdotes abound where physicians learn through the HIE of drugs being taken that the patient did not mention, past history of disease that could have caused complications, etc.

The HITECH Act was created specifically to stimulate the adoption of EHRs as "part of a modernized, interconnected, and vastly improved system of care delivery."[69] From the beginning, Meaningful Use provisions were developed with the understanding that EHRs on their own were not enough—interconnectivity was a requirement to meet the ultimate goals of improved quality and safety at an affordable price. The information exchange Meaningful Use criterion in Stage 1 is a simple demonstration of shared clinical data with a separate legal entity; however, the criteria of the next two stages will rapidly accelerate to meet the vision of truly interconnected EHRs.

Alignment with Transformation Strategy

Implementation of EHRs in time and in a manner to receive Meaningful Use incentives from CMS is receiving tremendous attention in the industry today. However, it is important to remember that the HITECH Act and Meaningful Use is a means to an end. With healthcare costs skyrocketing and an aging population, some manner of payment reform is certain to happen. The answer to this dilemma from CMS is the Accountable Care Organization (ACO). "The goal of ACOs is to pay providers in a way that encourages them to work together, to pay providers in a way that does not encourage supplier induced demand, and to create an organization that is rewarded for providing high quality care."[70] In order for this stated goal to be achieved—via ACOs or some other structure—information that improves care coordination and can accurately assess quality outcomes will be foundational. The ability for providers within the same medical trading area to share information and coordinate care (the notion of "co-opetition") will enable all to share in the rewards associated with improved outcomes.

Accountability

HIE strategies in the beginning stages (i.e., for the next several years) will be very reliant upon the application of technology to the caregiving entities. CIOs will clearly have accountabilities for this strategy. However, the more difficult aspects of the strategy surround the complexities of legal, privacy and local healthcare community politics and will require not just technology leadership but operational leadership from the rest of the 'C' suite" to achieve success.

Processes that Will Impact Realizing this Benefit

The processes that will be impacted with HIEs involve both the creation of meaningful, sharable data, as well as caregiving workflows that have imbedded the use of data that previously have been unavailable.

1. **Patient Identification and Indexing:** Ensuring information follows patients as they navigate the multiple sites of care will require very robust patient indexing and record matching. This requires not only an Enterprise Master Patient Index (EMPI) that creates one identifier within affiliated entities but also expands to a Community Master Patient Index (CMPI) that can then connect patient information that may come from unaffiliated entities. This underlying process and technology must become an industry-wide competency.

Keys to Success:
1. Widespread adoption through process workflow orientation
2. Transparent governance
3. Narrowly and clearly defined goals
4. Multiple services aimed at various participants in the value chain
5. Advanced value-added services

2. **Registration/scheduling:** Initially HIEs will play a valuable role in the registration and scheduling process in multiple ways. Demographic data can be shared between providers, alleviating the need to ask the patient multiple times for the same data and/or duplicating insurance verification and pre-certifications. Eventually as the exchanges mature, the expectation is that providers seamlessly move a patient through care settings with only one administrative interaction.

3. **Patient Assessment:** The intake and assessment of patients will be greatly enhanced when information about previous treatments, test results, problem lists and medications are available. The process will become verifying and updating rather than gathering. Though the result should be more accurate information, it will create new issues around data retention, data ownership and true source of information.

4. **Emergency Department (ED):** Having access to recent results in the patient record from other providers has created a new process in the ED that begins with looking up the patient in the HIE to gain context before starting treatment. The nature of EDs—treating emergent or urgent problems without previous exposure to the patient—historically has resulted in duplicate testing and/or treatments without understanding of the patient's past care. With availability of the patient's history, ED caregivers can now be more closely aligned and involved with the patient's specific treatment plans rather than the historical process of treat/stabilize and refer.

5. **Medication Reconciliation:** Understanding the medications a patient is currently taking is a truly difficult task. Patients do not remember, do not know and may not follow prescribed directions. Trying to capture this information usually involves multiple caregivers, phone calls to pharmacies and even visual inspection of medications brought to the care setting. With an information exchange, the process will have a greater chance of creating accurate lists as caregivers will have

access at a minimum to what has been prescribed. The reconciliation will then be more focused on adherence. While not fool proof, it eliminates some of the conflicting, incomplete data seen today.

6. **Clinical Documentation:** The adage "garbage in, garbage out" will apply to any information exchange. The importance of robust clinical documentation is becoming greater as more caregivers and even patients will have access to the data. It is critical, therefore, that the clinical documentation process is highly standardized, complete and accurate. Those data elements that will cross to others in the information exchange must be reliable if the HIE is to succeed.

Best Practice

Health information exchanges come in many different forms of ownership, objective, scope, functionality and funding source (see Table 4-1).

TABLE 4-1: Health Information Exchange Models.

Ownership Options	Potential Objectives	Scope/ Coverage	Functionality	Funding Sources
Public	Provide infrastructure	State, multi-state	Delivery of test results	Government grants
Public/private partnership	Standard setting/ governance	State	Hosting electronic health records	Member dues
Private for profit	Clearinghouse	Region (e.g., county, service area)	Proactive decision support (e.g., alerts)	Subscription
Private non-profit	Exchange and store data for improved outcomes (e.g., population health, cost, quality)	Affiliated entities	Data repository for analysis	Cost savings
		Specific patient population (e.g., registries, insured groups)		

The many variations of HIE models allow each initiative to be structured in a manner that best serves its intended purpose. For example, exchanges that are intended to be standards setting and infrastructure support are generally publicly owned and operated with state-supported funding. Those that are geared to improving efficiency of resources (i.e., lower cost) tend to be owned by health plans and integrated health systems and are provided free or with minimal fees to encourage broad inclusion by providers.

No one model has emerged as a single best practice, as the purpose and objective of the initiatives still vary widely. However, common themes around achieving ROI have emerged. Successful HIEs:

- Do not rely on grants to sustain operations; rather, utilize the money to expand capabilities or coverage.
- Collect fees from all participants in the HIE—including physicians, understanding that consumers of the information receive value, as well as distributors.
- Include payers in the financial support structure. Though payers as yet are not major financial contributors of financial support (excluding the impact of HIE technology firm ownership), most successful and more mature HIEs recognize the potential savings in healthcare costs will ultimately accrue to the payers. This particularly will be apparent as value-based and risk-sharing payment structures become more prevalent.

Conclusion

HIEs are not a new phenomenon. The concept of exchanging data between healthcare service providers to improve care and reduce costs is fairly easy to digest. However, because the current health system in the United States is characterized by a fragmented supply base and third-party payers who are not the consumers of the service, achieving the goal of seamless, robust exchange of health information has been very difficult to attain. Furthermore, if attained it has been very difficult to sustain over long periods of time. While the current environment is not filled with many success stories, the goal should not be abandoned. Examples of success do exist and can be replicated.

> "The true return on health IT rests in infrastructure that will assimilate relevant clinical data, build information-sharing links, and transform clinical workflow. These are the elements of a robust and secure Health Information Exchange (HIE) network."
>
> **J.Marc Overhage, MD, PhD**
> **President & CEO, Indiana HIE**

Using these examples as road maps, successful and sustainable HIEs, should exhibit the following characteristics:

1. Multi-faceted stakeholders from all aspects of the value chain (i.e., providers, payers, labs, public health, etc.).
2. Clearly defined and narrowly focused goals.
3. Strong governance and trust among stakeholders.
4. Advanced, value-added services for multiple stakeholders.
5. Process, workflow orientation rather than simple technology deployment.

The healthcare industry in the United States will change significantly over the next decade and IT will be one of the critical enablers of this change. Members of the value chain that are able to work through the barriers and achieve the potential benefits from an integrated information exchange will be the ones still standing when the health reform dust clears.

Strategy: *Population Health Management*

Susan Irby

Introduction

Population Health Management, as opposed to Public Health, refers to disease management of patients with specific, chronic conditions, such as diabetes or congestive heart failure. Research organizations, along with CMS, have studied the cost associated with caring for these patients and it is considerable. Of the $1.3 trillion spent on healthcare in the United States in 2007 for the non-institutionalized population, almost half was for treatment of chronic conditions.[71] There has been a great deal of research conducted around populations with these conditions and evidence collected to identify best practices for care from prevention to screening/early detection to care delivery in both the ambulatory and acute settings. Three key components to managing at-risk populations are: 1) educating and engaging the patients in their care, encouraging adherence to treatment plans; 2) actively monitoring the patient's health and treating according to evidence-based guidelines; and 3) coordinating care across settings to ensure the most timely and appropriate interventions.[72] Clinical decision support can play an important role in all three aspects of managing patient populations.

What Is the Pay-Off/Outcome?

Effective population health management will not only save the nation's healthcare delivery system dollars by minimizing acute care episodes and expensive treatments but will result in healthier individuals, longer productive life spans and higher quality of life. Use of Clinical Decision Support strategies and rules will enable more effective disease-specific management of patients and their care through patient education and monitoring, application of best practice clinical protocols and coordinating care between providers (see Figure 4-12). Examples of patient

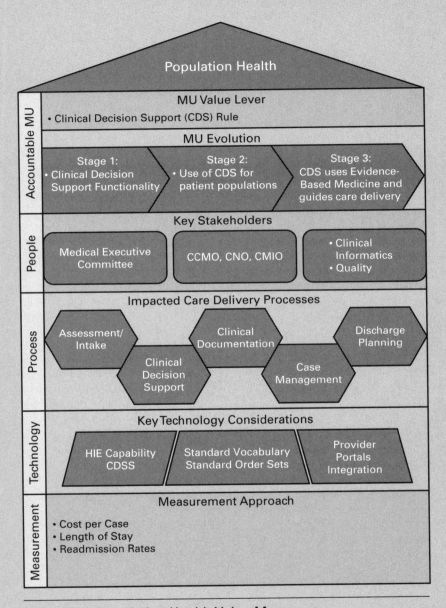

FIGURE 4-12: Population Health Value Map.

populations and the ways in which incorporation of clinical decision support rules can impact care include:

- **Diabetes:** For these patients, building reminders into the workflow for primary care providers to make sure regularly scheduled lab work (e.g., A1C [test for blood glucose] levels) occur and are reviewed, along with other diabetic monitoring (foot check, eye exams) can have a significant impact on outcomes. Ensuring these activities take place will reduce the risk of other complicating conditions such as renal failure, heart disease, blindness and gangrene/amputation due to wounds. In addition, by managing care of these patients, unnecessary hospitalizations can be avoided.

- **Congestive Heart Failure:** These patients run the risk of acute episodes (hospitalization/re-admission). Key therapy for heart failure patients is ACE inhibitors (angiotensin-converting enzyme inhibition), and diet controls, especially around salt and fluid intake. In addition, exercise plays a key role in significantly improving quality of life. Development of clinical decision support rules to ensure medication, diet and exercise activities are taking place in the home setting can help caregivers maintain contact with patients and confirm adherence to care plans.

- **Patients Receiving Anticoagulants:** Patients who have had an acute episode involving stroke, thrombosis, etc., have a simple but critical testing and management protocol around blood thinners. Clinical decision support rules can be implemented to remind providers of the need to perform testing for current levels of coagulation at the appropriate intervals.[73] These rules can be designed to be utilized at transitions of care when medication lists are reviewed and reconciled, as well as in each care setting at the frequency that best demonstrated practice indicates.

Meaningful Use Value Lever

Many of the Meaningful Use requirements impact improvement of population health; areas such as monitoring body mass index (BMI), and smoking status, as well as demonstration of quality care through metrics such as cholesterol screening, blood pressure screening and monitoring of A1C levels. Clinical decision support serves as a "lynchpin" in providing guidance for best demonstrated practice in delivery of care and assuring that these basic activities critical to managing population health are carried out regardless of care setting. Population health will also rely on improvement of quality, not only in the provider and hospital arena but with long-term care, home health and other care settings.

Alignment with Transformation Strategy

Employment of Clinical Decision Support and Evidence-based Medicine will aid in delivering the most effective care for patients. Furthermore, as reimbursement mechanisms continue to evolve and payment is based on outcomes, the ability to demonstrate that best practice is incorporated in care planning, care delivery and care coordination will be a key component of receiving more favorable reimbursement rates.

Organizations must be able to demonstrate that they employ a rules-based approach to delivery of care and that their approach spans across the care continuum. Where the organization does not have specific capabilities (e.g., long-term care), they must be able to clearly define the crosswalks to the key care components outside their capabilities that will ultimately serve to close the loop between acute care, the primary care provider and other community resources.

Accountability

Management of the health of specific populations is an evolving science. While a multidisciplinary team for each cohort (e.g., diabetes, congestive heart failure, etc.) will be necessary to provide day-to-day oversight, the ultimate responsibility should lie with either the CQO or CMIO. At the next level, Case Management and Clinical Informatics should be providing support to execute on specific actions needed to coordinate the most effective care across settings.

Processes that Will Impact Realizing this Benefit

While the notion of population management implies that activity will occur across care settings, clearly defined processes to ensure identification of and appropriate treatment protocols for select patient populations will contribute to effective management of these populations.

1. **Assessment/Intake:** Understanding primary and secondary diagnoses, as well as what underlying conditions a patient may have when presenting for care will help determine the correct pathways and protocols, including standard order sets and accompanying clinical decision support rules that are most appropriate for the patient.
2. **Care Planning:** Applying clinical decision support rules and evidence-based medicine to the plan of care will result in improved outcomes. At a minimum, care planning across care venues must demonstrate understanding of primary diagnosis, key co-morbidities, and appropriate interventions in order to ensure the appropriate plan of care is developed.
3. **Clinical Documentation:** Clear, consistent clinical documentation using structured problem lists, standard nomenclatures and code sets

will be essential to aligning an individual patient's situation with best demonstrated practice for the purpose of ensuring the best possible outcome. By identifying key diagnoses and conditions, evidence-based protocols can be identified and employed to ensure the appropriate treatment and monitoring occurs.

4. **Case Management:** The ability to understand the standard care pathway, expected interventions and resource consumption is critical in terms of inpatient days (including level of care), and additional tests/therapies necessary to move from acute care to lower acuity settings including long-term care, home health and others. Case management will need to extend past the acute care phase of an episode with follow-up phone calls and other interventions by case managers to ensure that patients are adhering to their treatment plan.

5. **Discharge Planning:** In conjunction with case management, planning the transition to the next care venue (including to the patient's home) will be critical in ensuring the best possible outcomes for the patient. Use of clinical decision support can help guide where and when the patient is placed, based on next level of care needed.

Best Practice

Best practice around clinical decision support will continue to evolve as organizations begin to attest for Stage 1 and move to Stages 2 and 3. The transition from implementation of a single clinical decision support rule in Stage 1 to using clinical decision support rules around specific patient populations to better manage their health will be critical to not only achieving accountable Meaningful Use but to positively impacting patient populations at risk. Key best practices to keep in mind as clinical decision support rules are being developed and implemented include:

- **Employ Robust Clinical Decision Support Capabilities:** While the discussion in this section has been around using information to manage patient populations, the clinical decision support technology to

Keys to Success:
1. Incorporation of evidence-based medicine rule sets
2. Collaborative approach to medical decision making
3. Defined desired outcomes by patient population

assist in planning and delivery of care should include the following functionalities: medication dosing support, order facilitation, point-of-care alerts and reminders, relevant information display, expert systems (artificial intelligence and evidence-based medicine) and workflow support.[74]

- **Focus on Utilization of Evidence-Based Medicine:** To manage population health, clinical decision support must use condition-specific order sets, condition-specific treatment protocols and transfer-specific order sets based on research. While organizations can develop their own rules, most find it is more practical (and less time-consuming) to purchase "off-the-shelf" rules and use them as a starting point. Those rules can then be customized to fit the organization's clinical operations. As comparative effectiveness research is disseminated, the capabilities (and accompanying processes) to update clinical decision support rules will be necessary to ensure that the current prevailing clinical best practice is driving care for the patient.

- **Incorporate Quality Improvement in Development of Clinical Decision Support Rules:** As organizations learn and grow with regards to measurement of specific quality indicators, they will identify ways to change their workflow and clinical decision making to improve outcomes. In performing a root cause analysis (or other technique) to determine reasons that a particular quality-based measure did not reach 100 percent success, opportunities for incorporating clinical decision support rules will become apparent. For example, a prescription for anticoagulants at discharge for stroke patients can be built into standardized order sets and alerts and reminders built into the EHR so that clinicians will not have to "remember" to do so themselves. Just as processes can be hardwired into technology, so can quality. Similarly reminders for routine screenings such as for cholesterol can be built into a provider's flow sheet to ensure screening for those patients who should be screened.

Conclusion

Managing Population Health can help slow the growth of overall costs to the national healthcare delivery system. At the same time, effective population health management allows patients (the population) to live healthier, longer and more productive lives because conditions are being monitored and managed on a proactive basis, rather than waiting for acute episodes to present.

The ability to develop and build evidence-based rules into the clinical workflow through clinical decision support tools in all care settings will provide many benefits: disease prevention, early screening and detection, focused risk management through medication and/or behavior modification and avoidance of hospitalizations/emergency visits. Through clinical decision support, the opportunity to improve population health can finally be realized.

Strategy: *Public Health*

Susan Irby

Introduction

Public Health, as opposed to Population Health, focuses on improving the overall health of a specific country or on improving health on a global basis. The modern Public Health movement got its start during the industrial revolution in "sanitary reform." Activities intended to protect the population at large included safe water supply, eradication of vectors (rats and other disease carries) and the development of vaccines and inoculation. In 1948, the World Health Organization (part of the United Nations) defined public health as: "A state of complete physical, mental, and social well-being and not merely the absence of disease or infirmity" (1948).[75]

While much of the healthcare delivery system in the United States today focuses on "healing"—acute care, chronic disease management and other interventions once a condition is present, Public Health focuses on prevention, management of risky behaviors and mitigating environmental factors in order to encourage wellness (see Figure 4-13). The HITECH Act addresses both the treatment and wellness aspects of health and healthcare.

What Is the Pay-Off/Outcome?

Successful execution of Public Health initiatives are aimed at improving the overall health of all Americans. Healthy People 2020 (this decade's sequel to the successful Healthy People 2010) is a program sponsored by the Department of Health and Human Services. It provides evidence-based, national objectives over a ten-year horizon for improving the health of all Americans,[76] with the specific nationwide outcomes of:

- **Improving Health Status:** Areas of focus include general health status, including life expectancy/healthy life expectancy, years of potential life lost (YPLL), physically and mentally unhealthy days, self-assessed health status, limitation of activity and chronic disease prevalence.

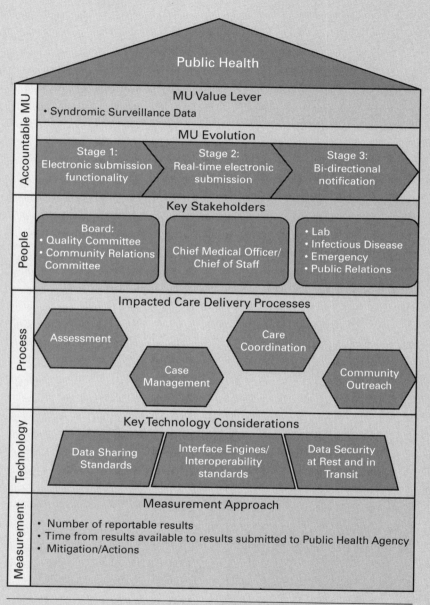

FIGURE 4-13: Public Health Value Map.

- **Improving Health-Related Quality of Life and Well-Being:** This multi-dimensional concept includes measures related to physical, mental, emotional and social functioning and focuses on the impact health status has on quality of life.[77]

- **Advancing Determinants of Health:** These include policymaking at the federal, state and local level around issues as varied as tobacco taxation and seat belt use in automobiles; social determinants such as employment status, education, transportation, crime; physical factors including quality of air and water; access to healthcare; behavioral factors such as tobacco and alcohol use; and biological/genetic factors.
- **Reducing Disparities:** Healthy People 2020 strives to improve the health across racial, ethnic, gender and socioeconomic groups.
- **Prevention:** Implicit in Healthy People 2020 are actions around screening and prevention. One of the Meaningful Use Criteria centers around reporting immunization status to state immunization registries. Other non-public health objectives related to public health include recording smoking status and charting BMI.
- **Biosurveillance:** The ability to rapidly become aware of outbreaks such as H1N1, SARS or other potential pandemic instances is critical to maintaining public health. The earlier that at-risk or infected populations are identified and isolated, the lower the risk to the remaining population at large.

Meaningful Use Value Lever

Public Health is the anchor point of the Meaningful Use Health Policy goal to improve Population and Public Health. As stated in the final rule, one of the care goals is around the ability of hospitals and providers to communicate to public health agencies in areas such as immunization status, lab results and syndromic surveillance data. While immunization registries are well-established and disease registries (e.g., cancer and cardiology) are emerging, the potential for sharing data around syndromic events (i.e., communicable diseases such as H1N1 and AIDS) will have significant impact in identifying outbreaks and potentiality limiting the spread of disease.

The ability to have bi-directional communications between providers (both hospitals and practices) and public health agencies will reduce response times to react to critical public health events such as infectious disease outbreaks.

Alignment with Enterprise Strategy

The principles associated with Public Health seem diametrically opposed to the current notion of caring for patients in an acute care or ambulatory setting, conducting volumes of diagnostic tests and delivering therapies. As the reimbursement mechanisms shift not only to bundled payments (in which there is no "per test" or "per admission" payment), but to paying for outcomes over time, the concept of paying for wellness will become more prevalent. Acute care organizations must determine their role in this new landscape and adjust their strategies to ensure their participation in the new reimbursement arena.

All organizations must be prepared to deal with communicable disease outbreaks. The incorporation of IT to identify these situations and communicate across organizations will be critical in minimizing the impact on public health.

Accountability

Acute care organizations often do not have a leadership role that focuses on the tenets of public health. There may be physicians who specialize in infectious disease, but they may not necessarily be able to address the entire gamut of Public Health. This is one of the areas where a new responsibility must be established and assigned. Medical Staff Leadership may be the best area in which to assign this responsibility.

Processes that Will Impact Realizing this Benefit

1. **Assessments:** Both physician assessments (history and physical, updating of Problem List) and nursing/other clinical assessments play a key role in identifying issues related to public health. These include identification of risky behaviors and conditions (smoking, alcohol, obesity), as well as exposure to environmental risks. In the case of syndromic surveillance, initial assessment is key to identifying potential infectious disease issues.

2. **Case Management:** Patients within an organized care setting can have their condition (including critical lab results) documented and communicated to the appropriate health agencies. While this is typically a paper process now, most EHR vendors are providing the capability to send the same information electronically.

3. **Community Outreach:** Hospitals, ambulatory sites and public health agencies will all participate in community health drives around flu shots, mobile mammography units, health fairs, cholesterol screenings and other activities that serve as vehicles to build awareness and achieve screening and prevention goals.

4. **Care Coordination:** Patients who need ongoing care coordination (those with a condition that requires ongoing monitoring) can be identified and care plans developed for optimal outcomes.

Best Practice

The ultimate intent for syndromic surveillance, as well as other Public Health initiatives, is to have real-time, bi-directional communications so that local caregivers can be apprised of public health situations in a timely manner. At this time, capabilities are limited, but the infrastructure is being put in place. The National Association for Public Health Information Technology (NAPHIT) is a national non-profit organization that provides leaders in Public Health IT with a venue to exchange ideas and experiences, discuss and shape current public health information policy and learn about tools and technologies that help them better support public health.[78]

Conclusion

Technology is critical in real-time submission of reportable conditions (such as H1N1) to agencies. This allows better understanding of the spread of these diseases/conditions. Technology will continue to evolve to allow bi-directional communication of information. This will allow hospitals and physicians to be aware of outbreaks on a more timely basis and deploy interventions to mitigate spread of disease.

Strategy: *Clinical Research*

Kevin Martin

Introduction

The first trial using properly randomized treatment and control groups was carried out in 1948 by the Medical Research Council and involved the use of streptomycin to treat pulmonary tuberculosis.[79] Since this time, clinical research has become much more structured with strict oversight and regulations while aiming to advance medical knowledge and the health of the patient.

As medical advances increase at an ever-increasing velocity, the ability to conduct trials in a timely manner has become more difficult. Finding the right subjects for trials and engaging physicians in the research requires the compilation and management of significant amounts of data that are not easily accessible or manageable. Recording patient demographics (age, race, gender, etc.) in the EHR is the first step in better organizing the patient information in an efficient way to use for research (see Figure 4-14). Healthcare is just now moving from a paper-based system in significant numbers, which will support the ability to access previously untapped resources and hopefully reverse the trend of increasing time to bring new treatments to market.

What Is the Pay-Off/Outcome?

By utilizing one of the fundamental Meaningful Use objectives, recording patient demographics, the ability to sift through thousands of paper medical records stored in unconnected file drawers suddenly becomes a much less intense resource requirement for the clinical research process.

- **Expansion of Patient Pool for Clinical Trials:** Currently, clinical trials are conducted using small populations developed by the researcher's ability to find relevant patient data. With the use of basic patient demographics, clinical researchers can quickly narrow the field based on age, gender and ethnicity. As the EMR and the data contained

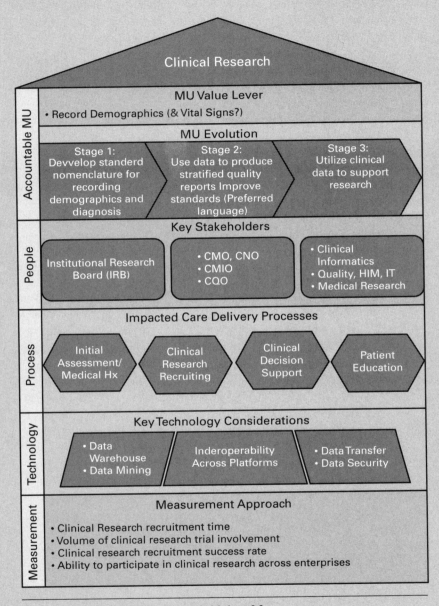

FIGURE 4-14: Clinical Research Value Map.

within it expand, the researcher can continue to save valuable time by reducing the field of patients considered. The University of Colorado Health Sciences Center found that 86 percent of all trials fail to enroll on time and nearly 90 percent of study days beyond the original study timetable are due to not recruiting subjects on time.[80] In the end, the EMR will drastically reduce costs associated with a provider's ability to identify appropriate patients for clinical research and improve their ability to participate in clinical trials.

- **Patient Stratification:** The ability to more quickly stratify a patient population will also greatly improve the statistical power of a study. As stated by the National Institutes of Health for Clinical Trials, *"The number of patients enrolled in a study has a large bearing on the ability of the study to reliably detect the size of the effect of the study intervention. The larger the sample size or number of participants in the trial, the greater the statistical power."*[81]

- **Correlation with Patient demographics:** This is but one example of data commonly available as structured data in EHRs for Meaningful Use criteria, as there are a multitude of additional benefits that can correlate to clinical research. For example, providers can also use:
  - Problem List.
  - Medication List.
  - Medication Allergy List.
  - Vital Signs.
  - Smoking Status.

Meaningful Use Value Lever

The underlying premise of recording demographics is a foundation on which to share the most basic patient information across the healthcare continuum. If an organization cannot succeed with this criterion, then there is little hope for the initiative at large. Correctly capturing patient demographics assists clinical research, which is part of the HITECH Act goals to improve Population and Public Health and to reduce disparities. In addition, this information will assist in obtaining robust data for comparative effectiveness research, allowing identification of disparities in care and pinpointing areas that need funding.

Alignment with Transformation Strategy

The end goal is to improve patient health over the long term by reducing the research cycle to determine root causes, optimal treatment and best practices. By recording the most basic patient data and incorporating additional data from other Meaningful Use metrics, the organization will be capable of building a more robust database around its patient population.

As research moves from academic settings to the community, organizations looking to the future recognize that a well-developed EHR enables a more efficient method to conduct clinical research. However, these organizations also realize it is much more:

- There is the opportunity to build more complex patient care models using clinical data to estimate the prevalence of various conditions and various rates of complications.
- It can also generate the ability to develop outcome reports closer to real-time care for clinicians using this information on various intermediate process measures or actual health outcomes.
- Using Clinical Decision Support, the organization has the ability to develop real-time interventions or disease management programs using the database to identify patients in various disease states or within certain parameters who are eligible for specific treatments or tests. This can also be directly linked with patient communication and patient education.

Ultimately these forward-looking organizations aim to structure a system supporting the EHR in a way that allows the system itself to run research queries that go beyond human intelligence to test theories. This information will then be fed back into the clinical care process directly at the time of care to provide real-time clinical decision support.

Accountability

Meaningfully used EHRs will provide the framework for organizations to participate and apply clinical research in ways not possible in the past. Ideally, given the relationship to institutional research boards (IRBs), accountability for this strategy will fall to medical staff leadership—typically, the head of the IRB. They will need support from leaders that have responsibility for clinical decision support, research support and quality.

Processes that Will Impact Realizing this Benefit

1. **Clinical Research Screening:** The entire process of sifting through thousands of disconnected paper charts showing only a very specific portion of the population to find the appropriate candidates for clinical trials will be streamlined. It will not completely disappear until paper records are eliminated and a great majority of providers are using a fully functioning EHR across the community, but it will continue to become easier as the EHR is developed.

2. **Clinical Research Follow Up:** Utilizing the EHR within the enterprise will enable simpler post-marketing surveillance studies identifying patients who received certain medications or combinations of medications or specific procedures and looking for increases in the incidence of adverse events or outcomes. Utilizing patient demographics and associated Meaningful Use measures will allow for much easier patient tracking and overall data mining to support clinical research before, during and after trials are conducted.

3. **Clinical Decision Support:** As the electronic use of clinical research grows, so too will its integration with clinical decision support. The results of research can be linked to information filtered within the system by select criteria (e.g., demographics, vital signs, medications) allowing specific information to be shared with clinicians during the time of care.

4. **Patient Education:** The patient education process would be closely linked with clinical decision support, so as specific data are entered on the patient during time of diagnosis or treatment, an alert may arise for clinicians informing them the patient may be eligible to take part in a clinical trial. Furthermore, the demographic information can be used to follow up with a patient with automatic communication regarding specific information about the clinical research.

Best Practice

Best practice for clinical research will vary widely between "bench" operations (pure research facilities), academic medical centers and community-based practices. However, there are common themes:

- **Patient Identification:** Physicians across different settings can be alerted to patients' eligibility for a trial through sharing of demographic and other data. Some medical practices, such as that of

Keys to Success:
1. The ability to map data across enterprises until standardized nomenclature is created for data collection
2. Develop the EHR with clinical research in mind as an integral part of improving health
3. Incorporate clinical decision support to manage dissemination of information

Holston Medical Group (HMG) in Kingsport, Tennessee, use their EHRs to increase the volume of clinical trials they are involved with, thus increasing revenue to the practice.[82] The EHR can enable providers more efficient management of the clinical trials, which allows time to be involved in more research and clinical trials.

- **Clinical Monitoring:** Availability of lab results and qualitative data for patients enrolled in clinical trials will assist in lowering rates of protocol violations and faster reporting of adverse events. Protocol violations occur when a patient becomes ineligible after being involved in a trial; one common occurrence is patients taking medications prescribed by a different physician (unaware of their involvement in the trial) that adversely affects or invalidates results of the trial. In addition, monitoring of trials from a demographic perspective will help correlate reasons why people go off a trial. It could be social issues (getting a ride to the physician's office) or non-tolerance of the drug.

Conclusion

Value comes to the clinical research process when patients eligible for studies can be quickly and accurately identified. Success is most evident when physician participation increases and required levels of clinical trial subjects can quickly be identified and recruited. These two improvements can reduce trial timeframes and broaden the populations able to participate. Both will aid in the quantity and quality of clinical trial outcomes at a time when scientific breakthroughs, particularly biomedical breakthroughs, are occurring at a dizzying rate.

Technology is going to be a key enabler in improving the clinical trial process. The ability to create "virtual" cohorts of patients through interoperable EHRs can allow trials to be conducted without regard to geographic, socio-economic or provider affiliation to academic centers. Diversifying the trial subjects and physician monitors will bring robustness to trials that today may be lacking. This breakthrough opportunity will exist if the achievement of Meaningful Use is viewed as the springboard to future capabilities rather than the end goal.

Strategy: *Privacy and Security*

Bryant Hoyal

Introduction

The groundbreaking shift in health IT privacy and security came with the 1996 passage of the Health Insurance Portability and Accountability Act (HIPAA). This legislation addressed a number of issues including the lack of standard uniform rules for security, the protection of health insurance during job transitions, the provision for national standards for electronic transactions and the establishment of national provider identifiers. An overarching accomplishment of the HIPAA law was to replace the multiple overlapping and uncoordinated federal, state and local acts with a national standard for privacy and security.

The scope of privacy protection under HIPAA was expanded with the 2009 passage of the HITECH Act following criticism that the privacy laws had not been rigorously enforced. The HITECH Act outlines objectives that hospitals and providers are required to meet in order to demonstrate achievement of Meaningful Use, receive incentive payments and avoid penalties. One of these required objectives stipulates that hospitals and providers must protect electronic health information maintained in the EHR by following a two-step process: conduct a security risk assessment (see Figure 4-15) and implement corrections for any identified security deficiencies. In addition, the legislation extended the provisions of HIPAA to business associates of covered entities, imposed new breach notification requirements and implemented new rules for the accounting of disclosures of a patient's health information.

What Is the Pay-Off/Outcome?

Ensuring privacy and security is considered a prerequisite component of any process or system involving health information. However, even

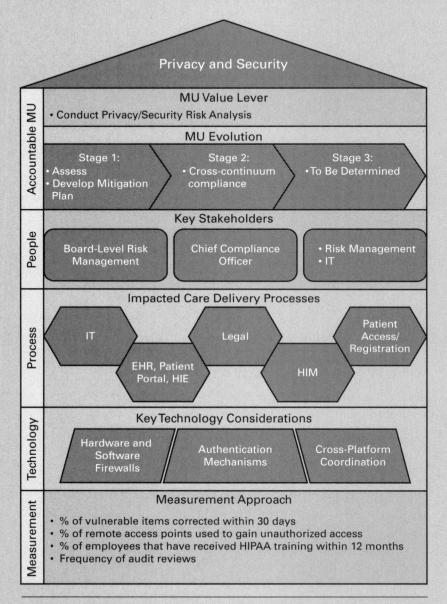

FIGURE 4-15: Privacy and Security Value Map.

though it is something organizations "have to do," there are substantial benefits to consider:

- **Building a Foundation of Trust within the Patient Community:** Patient confidence in the security of their personal data is critical to encourage sharing of information. This basis of trust can lead to greater adoption of patient engagement tools such as patient portals, secure electronic messaging, online scheduling and wellness mobile applications. These tools vary in purpose and include such pay-offs as an increased focus on prevention, better adherence to treatment plans, improved patient outcomes and reduced utilization of high-cost emergency services.

- **Streamlined Formats for Data Interchange:** Implementing HIPAA administrative simplification standards, including standard formats for electronic data interchange, paves the way for provider organizations to automate the payer communication process. Streamlining this process provides considerable pay-offs including greater accuracy of data, timeliness of information and fewer resources required to achieve transfer of data.

- **Improved Clinical Decision Making:** Privacy and security measures work to prevent situations where inaccurate, incomplete or missing data are used for clinical decision making. Mitigating this risk reduces the adverse consequence of compromising patient care. Ensuring the right data about the right patient are available to the right care provider at the right time prevents data security issues that could lead to disastrous clinical outcomes.

- **Avoidance of penalties:** The penalties for non-compliance vary but can include negative legal judgments, implementing extensive (and expensive) corrective action plans, fines and public disclosures, not to mention the reputational damage and financial repercussions therein.

Meaningful Use Value Lever

The specific core objective for Privacy and Security that requires hospitals and providers to conduct a risk analysis and correct identified deficiencies is not new. CMS is reinforcing existing HIPAA requirements. Conducting a risk analysis and taking action to mitigate risks is part of the existing HIPAA legislation with which all Covered Entities are required to comply. By reiterating this basic requirement, requiring hospital attestation of its completion and layering on the additional components around business associates, accounting of disclosures and selling data, CMS is sending a signal of the importance of privacy and security.

Alignment with Transformation Strategy

Protecting the integrity of information used for clinical decision making is a fundamental part of providing optimal patient care. Therefore, identifying institutional vulnerabilities in data privacy and preventing avoidable violations are mission-critical activities that should become an integral part of an organization's comprehensive IT strategy, whether the technology is an EHR, patient portal, HIE, ancillary or other clinical or financial system.

Organizations that recognize the critical importance of privacy and security hardwire their approach to security by establishing a security management program, sponsoring it at an executive level, developing a risk management framework and prioritizing early detection. The risk management framework should encompass a wide-ranging scope of hardware, software, interfaces, networks and storage devices, involve a multi-disciplinary team of IT and end-user champions and may require tapping into the expertise of third-party specialty consultants or the use of automated specialty tools.

Accountability

Privacy and security of data in an environment of EHRs will create the need for strong leadership in compliance management. Chief Compliance Officers, whether full- or part-time, will need to ensure policies and procedures are in place and followed, risks are constantly evaluated and audited, tools and technology adequately protect data and ongoing monitoring is proactive to catch breeches before they occur. In organizations that do not have legal counsel on staff, Risk Management must work with contracted legal services to ensure that the appropriate safeguards are in place to ensure compliance.

Processes that Will Impact Realizing this Benefit

Safeguarding sensitive data requires a culture of privacy and security throughout the organization. While all areas have the potential to be impacted, there are a few that are directly responsible for the protection of data:

1. **Health Information Management:** As stewards of patient data, Health Information Management (HIM) professionals should be ingrained in privacy and security processes. As the public point of access for health information, the Release of Information process should be a chief focus when assessing vulnerabilities. Given that the individual requesting the information is often someone other than the patient (such as a family member, legal representative, payer or other provider), a critical step is ensuring appropriate authorization

and consent. Policies and procedures should require all requests go through a central point of control that results in thorough documentation. In addition, HIM professionals must use proper data governance practices to ensure they are releasing the complete record, a task that becomes increasingly complex in the electronic environment.

2. **Information Technology:** Obviously there are considerable impacts to IT with protecting health information. Privacy and security practices and procedures should be foundational components of deployment plans for any technology that stores, retrieves, exchanges or maintains patient health information. Healthcare organizations often experience the competing demands of needing to protect health information with needing to use that information. As the gatekeeper to the electronic medical record, IT must find a balance to ensure data are simultaneously protected and used to benefit patient care.

3. **Patient Access and Registration:** The conception of a patient record occurs at registration. There are two critical components to ensuring accuracy during the registration process. First, proper physical identification practices prevent identity theft and related fraudulent activity. Second, accurate patient identity integrity practices work to make sure the right information is connected to the right patient.

4. **Legal:** The overlapping legislation around privacy and security is complex and the repercussions from negligence are substantial. With so much at risk, enterprise privacy management policies and practices should be under the review of legal counsel.

Best Practice

The healthcare industry has long been concerned with privacy and security of patient information. In some regards, it is one area that other industries have looked to for best practices. As EHRs become more widespread and data becomes increasingly available as a result, organizations should ensure best practices are consistently followed.

- **Awareness:** The 2010 HIMSS Security Study found that 30 percent of Business Associates are not even aware that the HITECH Act extended HIPAA to cover them.[83] The responsibility for outreach and education in this area falls to the Covered Entities. Best practice requires organizations to be proactive in their business associate relationships to ensure compliance.

Keys to Success:
1. Recognize the separate but complementary goals of privacy and security
2. Pursue highly visible executive sponsorship for privacy and security initiatives
3. Assign influential, effective leaders to manage work effort
4. Promote awareness organization-wide
5. Establish culture of accountability within end-user community
6. Continuously refine the process

- **Current Policies and Procedures:** Upon deeper review of the recently disclosed breeches, one contributing factor was that many of the provider organizations had not updated their policies and procedures in over eight years. Organizations following best practice are successful at operationalizing the process of reviewing policies and procedures, continuously assessing and updating them to reflect the current protocols and systems, holding team members accountable and methodically identifying risks and mitigating them.
- **Collaboration:** Provider organizations that are truly successful with privacy and security recognize that it is a collaborative effort combining people, process and technology. These organizations consider protecting their patients' health information to be a core competency and work to create a culture that reveres privacy and values patient trust.

Conclusion

The HIPAA and HITECH legislations provide some leeway to healthcare organizations on the mechanisms used to protect health information. Encryption is not explicitly required by the HITECH Act

"One of the [HHS's] guiding principles is that the benefits of health IT can only be fully realized if patients and providers are confident that electronic health information is kept private and secure."[84]

David Blumenthal, MD, MPP, former National Coordinator for Health Information Technology, U.S. Department of Health and Human Services (HHS)

or HIPAA. In fact, the final rule around certification indicates ONC's flexibility around standards for encryption algorithms to protect data security. Similarly, while two-factor authentication has been offered by CMS as a mechanism for protecting personal health information that is accessed remotely, it is not explicitly required. It is possible that both of these tools will be required in the future.

By layering legislation around privacy and security in multiple rules, CMS clearly wishes to make a point about the importance of these areas and is encouraging provider organizations to incorporate information security management into the programs and processes for all IT systems. To fully achieve the value from security-related initiatives, organizations must consider this to be more than a technical operation by defining a vision at the enterprise level as to the degree of protection of their patient's health information and by developing an enterprise-wide framework for continuous accountable achievement.

It has been clear in numerous research studies that, when it comes to healthcare information, patients trust their providers more than any other sources. According to an April 2011 report by the Institute for Health Technology Transformation, 58 percent of adults without a Personal Health Record would be interested in using one if offered by their hospital or medical practice, compared to 50 percent if offered by a payer and only 25 percent by Google, Microsoft or their employer.[85] Opportunistic organizations recognize their responsibility to maintain that trust. They leverage patient trust with patient engagement tools that lead to consumer loyalty, better clinical outcomes, reduced costs and competitive advantage.

Although privacy and security are obligatory requirements, thorough compliance protects an organization's investments in information technology, builds confidence within their physician, clinician and patient communities and allows them to maximize the value they receive from system implementation.

Chapter 5

Value Realization

Marla Crockett, Susan Irby, Kevin Martin and Vicki Miller

> *"If ever there was a time that innovative solutions are needed, we are in that time. One of the most visible examples of such innovation, and one that few people truly understand, is the profound impact of a successful implementation of an electronic medical record."*[86]
>
> David L. Bernd, FACHE, CEO, Sentara Healthcare, Norfolk, VA, and
> Peter S. Fine, FACHE, CEO, Banner Health in Phoenix, AZ

Value Maps do not replace detailed Meaningful Use Mitigation or IT Systems Mitigation Planning and Project Management. They provide a performance management system to ensure investment is managed and returns are realized. The Value Realization phase of the Value Management Process is the largest, most complex and most critical component to ensure enterprise success. It involves much of the work healthcare organizations are focused on today and includes the following components:

- Develop Decision-Making Structure and Assign Accountability.
- Design Process & Workflow.
- Develop Adoption Strategies.
- Implement IT Systems.

Develop Decision-Making Structure and Assign Accountability

Establishing an effective decision-making structure and assigning accountability is critical to achieving Accountable Meaningful Use and transforming the delivery of healthcare. Historic governance and management models focused on acute care operations and loose confederations of physicians connected through medical staff membership and medical executive committees will not provide the level of oversight and improvement in clinical quality, patient safety, resource consumption and other benefits described in the previous chapter. Decision-making structures must become patient-centered and incorporate perspectives from across the continuum of care delivery.

In previous books in this series, the topic of IT Governance has been addressed as a key success factor in realizing return on investment for health IT. Yet, many in the healthcare enterprise still consider the term governance to mean composition of and activities pertaining to an organization's Board of Directors/Trustees. For this discussion, Governance is defined as the decision-making process by which leaders achieve the organization's shared strategic vision by providing guidance to others, direct oversight, or primary execution of plans.[87] Additionally, we will address the topic of the necessary medical decision-making framework necessary to achieve Accountable Meaningful Use. There are a number of questions today's healthcare leaders may ask:

What Roles and Responsibilities Will Change?

Accountable care and Meaningful Use will require new levels of integrated decision making. For some period of time, physicians, hospital leaders and other healthcare professionals will have to balance volume-based decision making with new decisions directed at reducing resource consumption, incorporating evidence-based process standardization and value-based care delivery models. Specifically, roles will include:

- **Board of Directors/Board of Trustees:** In addition to existing fiduciary responsibilities, the board must serve as the final level of approval for enterprise strategies related to Meaningful Use and other healthcare reform initiatives. The initiatives will include not only IT purchases/implementations, but will also include development of:
  - New types of relationships with physicians, payers and other members of the healthcare community.
  - Strategies and plans for the exchange of health information within the enterprise, and external to the existing enterprise.
  - Expanded strategies to engage with patients and their families.
  - Redefined payment methods and structures, including:
    - ◦ Value-based purchasing.
    - ◦ Bundled payments.
    - ◦ Accountable care organizations.
    - ◦ Patient-centered medical homes and, increased public reporting.[88]

- **Health System (Hospital, Providers, Others) Administration/ Leadership:** Operational and clinical leadership must continue to focus day-to-day operations—providing quality patient care, while providing information and perspective regarding barriers for meeting overall and individual Meaningful Use objectives. At the same time, a vision for the healthcare enterprise of the future should be developed with specific strategic goals focused on reduction in variation, improved quality, reduced cost and expanded access to care. Healthcare leaders must work with front-line staff to redesign workflows to integrate Meaningful Use technologies and requirements in addition to leading the adoption of new care delivery philosophies (Patient Centered Care) and models of care.
- **Physician Leaders:** Physicians across the healthcare community must be engaged in strategic and clinical decisions. While the number of employed physicians is increasing significantly, this alone is not enough. Physicians must be truly integrated into leadership roles with common goals, value-targeted strategies and tools that support the desired level of transformation. A number of vehicles including co-management agreements, clinical institutes, management service organizations, physician-hospital organizations, physician leadership cabinets, etc., are being tested as the platform for clinical integration. Regardless of the structure, Figure 5-1 shows how physician leadership structures are necessary at many levels, including:[89]
  - Institutional physician leaders will be members of the executive leadership team, defining the strategic direction for the enterprise, defining the clinical direction for the enterprise in the new healthcare environment. Engaging physicians to lead and partner with the enterprise at all levels will result in more effective collaboration and decision making in the transformation journey.
  - Service line physician leaders will drive clinical decisions related to: use of current evidence for decision making, access to evidence/ research, defining clinical services for the enterprise, re-defining roles/responsibilities for engaging patients in managing their own care and the integration of clinical, operational and financial information for better decision making.
  - Front line physician leaders will drive clinical decisions such as: definition and maintenance of order sets, problem lists and clinical decision support rules. In addition they will play a key role in shaping the way in which health information is exchanged, in engaging patients in their care and in coordination of care across settings.

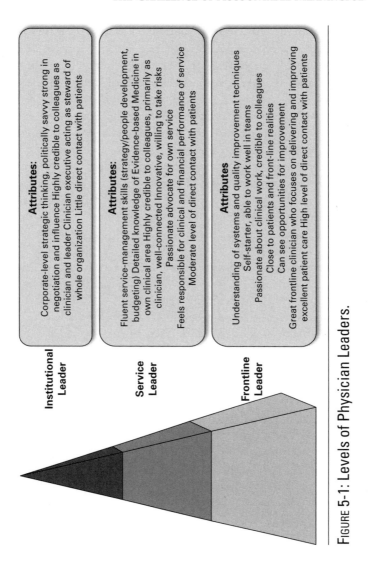

Institutional Leader

Attributes:
Corporate-level strategic thinking, politically savvy strong in negotiation and influence Highly credible to colleagues as clinician and leader Clinician executive acting as steward of whole organization Little direct contact with patients

Service Leader

Attributes:
Fluent service-management skills (strategy/people development, budgeting) Detailed knowledge of Evidence-based Medicine in own clinical area Highly credible to colleagues, primarily as clinician, well-connected Innovative, willing to take risks Passionate advocate for own service Feels responsible for clinical and financial performance of service Moderate level of direct contact with patients

Frontline Leader

Attributes
Understanding of systems and quality improvement techniques Self-starter, able to work well in teams Passionate about clinical work, credible to colleagues Close to patients and front-line realities Can see opportunities for improvement Great frontline clinician who focuses on delivering and improving excellent patient care High level of direct contact with patients

FIGURE 5-1: Levels of Physician Leaders.

- **Clinical Leaders (Nursing, Pharmacy, Others):** Front-line leaders with a role in the delivery of care must work in a collaborative fashion to make decisions about both clinical care delivery processes and the use of clinical, financial and operational information to make better clinical decisions for patients. Non-physician clinical leaders will need to collaborate with physician and administrative leaders to redefine how work (delivery of care) is done, the changes in care team roles/ responsibilities and how quality will be measured. Rather than just *meeting* Meaningful Use thresholds and requirements, consideration should be given to both up- and downstream implications. Decisions made in a vacuum may have unintended consequences on patient care within and outside the immediate enterprise.

- **The Healthcare Community:** In order to make truly effective, patient-centric decisions, providers and organizations outside the enterprise must be involved to help craft the future community health vision that reaches across care settings. The future vision for health must incorporate: population health requirements/demands, population health and wellness education, chronic disease management, integration of community services and the use of technology to coordinate care across the community. This includes local public health agencies, state agencies, non-affiliated community providers, long-term care and home health.

Who Will Have Ultimate Accountability?

Many healthcare organizations avoid accountability for value by using consensus decision-making approaches. With limited responsibility for results, and the ability to opt-out of voluntary technology adoption plans, it is not a surprise that healthcare is behind other industries in technology's ability to drive transformation. Additionally, healthcare comprises many complex processes. Most of these processes cross a number of functional areas. Since no one function owns the complete process, accountability is rarely assigned. More often than not, we find the accountability for Meaningful Use assigned to the CIO. Yet most CIOs agree they have limited input/responsibility for dissemination of evidence to impact clinical decision making, quality measurement, registration and other key processes impacting Meaningful Use.

At a tactical level, Meaningful Use teams should assign business and clinical owners with responsibility for key steps within Meaningful Use mitigation plans. At a broader more strategic level, accountability will have to be assigned to ensure that EHR deployment, process redesign and other change initiatives consider the goals of accountable care:

- Alignment of organizations, professionals and functional systems of care to improve the efficiency of care.
- Definition of a standard system of care across delivery systems and settings, providers, specialties, disciplines, programs and service lines.
- Delivery of care in the safest and least resource-intensive setting.
- Elimination of non-value adding interventions, procedures and workflows.
- Improvement in access to the continuum of care for designated population groups.

- Transition to a patient-centered approach to care where clinicians work with their patients to improve prevention and the overall management of their health.

What Types of Decision Should be Made?

Policy, procedure, participation, content and technology decisions related to Meaningful Use will need to be made within and across entities. Consideration needs to be given not only to the stakeholder groups that should be involved in making the decisions, but to the types of decisions being made. Key decisions include:[90]

- Enterprise strategies for clinical integration, patient engagement, quality improvement and patient safety.
- Health IT strategy in key areas such as HIE, personal health record (PHR) and EHR; what technology components will be used to meet Meaningful Use; the timing for implementing these technology components.
- Defining new care delivery models.
- New integrated care delivery processes (integration of process, workflows, technology and evidence-based practices).
- Conscious design of clinical care delivery processes/workflows and practices to decrease variation in care delivery.
- How performance and productivity measurement will need to be redefined.
- How clinical quality and outcomes will be measured and monitored.
- How reporting of clinical quality and performance across care settings and organizations will occur.
- How the organization will ensure that privacy and security requirements are met and that these are communicated to the patient.
- Timing for attestation for Stage 1 in light of requirements for Stages 2 and 3.

Critical for Stage 1 planning and decision making is not only the timing for Stages 2 and 3 but the decisions for both the way technology is implemented and the way processes around using the technology are designed. Focusing on Stage 1 only presents risks at two levels. First, the organization may not be prepared for later Meaningful Use stages within the legislated timeframes. Second, if value is not planned for, it will not occur.

Table 5-1 describes the relationship between the type of decisions that will need to be made as part of Accountable Meaningful Use and the key decision makers and decision-making bodies that must participate in the decision-making process.

TABLE 5-1: Decision Type by Stakeholder.

Example Decisions	Board	Executive Leadership	Physician Leadership	Clinical Leadership	Integrated Community
Enterprise strategies for clinical transformation	✓	✓	✓	✓	
Health IT strategy	✓	✓	✓		
Technology strategies to achieve Meaningful Use		✓			
Enterprise timing for attestation (EH and EP)		✓	✓	✓	
New care delivery models		✓	✓	✓	✓
Integrated care delivery processes design			✓	✓	
Strategies to reduce clinical care variation			✓	✓	
Performance and productivity measurement		✓	✓	✓	
Clinical quality and outcomes measurement		✓	✓	✓	✓
Care coordination strategies			✓	✓	✓
Meeting/monitoring privacy and security	✓	✓	✓	✓	✓
Timing for attestation for Stage 1 in light of requirements for Stages 2 and 3		✓	✓	✓	

What Should a Decision-Making Framework Include?

It is clear that success under high value healthcare requires providers to transform both the organization and delivery of care in ways that will benefit the successful provider system regardless of the ultimate form that Accountable Care Organizations may take.[91] The decision-making framework for the transformed healthcare delivery system should be designed as an amalgamation of the existing organizational leadership structure, integrating transformational decision making across the continuum and healthcare community. The new paradigm for decision making will require new relationships to be forged, innovation in leadership and a fundamental change in thinking about the delivery of healthcare.

To meet the Federal Trade Commission's definition of Clinical Integration, organizations must achieve efficiencies by monitoring and controlling quality, service and costs; selectively choosing physician participants; employing evidence-based practice standards and making a significant investment of monetary or human capital in infrastructure, including information technology.[92] Championing the future vision and leading the transformational change of the enterprise will be the primary focus of the leadership team.

Questions enterprise leaders must be able to ask and answer include:

- Have we engaged and partnered with our physician leaders?
- Have we collaborated with our physician partners to clearly define our future vision?
- Do we have the right participants at the table to lead us into the future?
- Do we have the right integrated network of providers to be able to service our population?
- Do we have the resolve and leadership necessary to define our future through improving clinical quality, enhancing access to care and reducing cost?

Shaping the decision-making environment around these questions will not only result in a unique structure for the enterprise but should also describe the role and relationship of the key groups. Some may already be established, while others may need to be created. As shown in Figure 5-2, key components include:

- An Executive Steering Committee focused on Accountable Meaningful Use. The governance structure will most likely be part of the organization's Clinical Integration Strategy and also work with new structures for Patient Centered Medical Homes, Accountable Care, etc. Different plans will exist for employed multispecialty groups, hospital-based physicians and other physician structures. Frequent reporting should occur to the board of the enterprise and address plans for interacting with external groups including payers, public health, health information exchanges, etc.

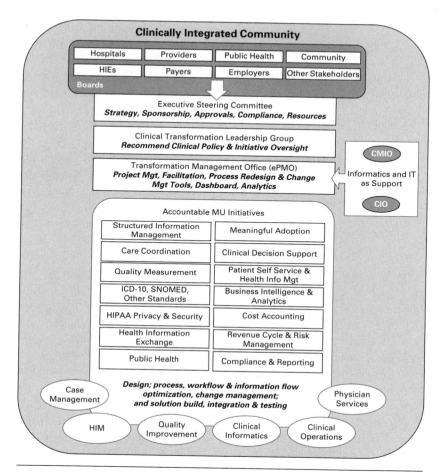

FIGURE 5-2: Integrated Decision-Making Framework.

- A Clinical Transformation Leadership Group should recommend policy and provide oversight of the transformation initiatives. Specific accountabilities should be assigned for evidence-based medicine, content design, standards development and care coordination approaches, etc. Key physician leaders should participate in the Clinical Transformation Leadership Group.
- A Program Management Office or, as many forward-thinking organizations are developing, the Enterprise Transformation Management Office (or "eTMO") has two primary purposes: 1) Deliver program management support to the organization by providing guidance in project management processes and methodologies in a manner that is

efficient, consistent and standardized, and 2) Provide mentoring and coaching to raise the project management, process redesign and change management (transformation) maturity level of the organization.

- Multidisciplinary project teams that draw upon cross-organizational expertise to redesign processes and information flows, and inform IT deployments in an efficient and effective manner. For example, a Structured Information Management team would impact CPOE, Problem Lists, Quality Reporting, Clinical Documentation and more.
- Key groups would be supplemented by feedback from internal advisory groups, as well as external groups such as local public health agencies, payers, local employers, etc. As clinical integration evolves, the Transformation governance and decision-making structure should change to match the needs of the health system.

Integrate Process and Technology Design

Lean and Six Sigma have been present in many other industries for several decades and have just become prevalent in healthcare over the past five to ten years. The programs are similar yet different, specifically:

- Lean is a systematic approach to reduce waste and inefficiencies.
- Six Sigma is a rigorous, data-driven process to reduce variation and eliminate errors.

Today these programs can be found in many healthcare facilities under a variety of different departments or descriptions—Quality, Performance Improvement, Process Improvement and even Project Management. Most of the initiatives are focused on functional improvement goals like Emergency Department throughput, surgical room turnover time or on-time case starts, magnetic resonance imaging (MRI) utilization, or improving core measures. While important, these initiatives are typically focused within departmental silos with limited integration with medical practices, cross continuum activities or IT implementations.

Many Information Services organizations, health IT consultants and health IT vendors recognize the impact of the technology on clinical workflows. There is an important distinction, however. Which type of workflow is being discussed? Horizontal workflows typically span across functions and involve redesign of human resources, processes and facilities. The inputs and outputs can be standardized, replicated and learned. Vertical workflows are focused on how the end user interacts with the technology (such as with EHR screens to enter required data), and how

> "Lean and Six Sigma have strong complementary strengths that are particularly useful for systematically developing healthcare service solutions."
>
> **National Association for Healthcare Quality**

the data flow between applications. The vertical process review typically does not look beyond how the system is used and often may not consider the upstream and downstream process impacts beyond the application.

Healthcare is implementing new technology at a more rapid pace than ever before. Unfortunately many healthcare providers are implementing technology on top of old or fragmented manual processes, which automates broken, inefficient work practices. When technology is implemented without regard to clinical workflow, caregivers create workarounds, become less efficient and increasingly frustrated, and spend more time with the computer and less time with the patients. This is clearly not the intent of the HITECH Act.

As healthcare evolves, the role of process improvement must expand beyond the walls of the hospital and its specific department. In his article, "Turning Doctors into Leaders," Thomas Lee says, "Healthcare teams can't view their purpose as time-limited or focused on one project." Organizations need a "culture of process improvement and the disciplined use of its methods, such as Lean management, data collection, brainstorming intervention and impact analysis—and a long-term commitment to applying them."[93] As the criteria in Stage 2 and 3 expands, the future of Lean and Six Sigma in healthcare will be focused on the efficient and effective flow of information using technology to support clinicians and care processes across multiple care delivery venues.

To facilitate adoption, organizations should consider aligning process redesign and EHR implementation activities as a part of the technology deployment. There are three major components to consider when integrating clinical processes with IT:

- The interaction between user and computer to enter information.
- The ability for the technology to share information and integrate with other technology (within and beyond the organization).
- The interaction with the user and computer to extract data and information to create knowledge.

The Integrated Process and Technology Approach (IPTA) is designed to follow the delivery of care to a patient across the organization from admission to discharge (horizontally) and not focus on the system or department solely (vertically). IPTA looks at how those involved in or impacted by the process will interact with the technology to carry out their responsibilities efficiently and effectively. By doing this, the organization will be able to develop a complete picture, not only capturing the right data at the right time, but also sharing this information with the right caregivers at the right time in the right format.

Defining Impacted Processes

The first step is to define the processes that will be impacted with the implementation of new technology. Questions to ask when defining the processes include:

- What patient care activities are supported by the application?
- Who will be interacting with the application to provide patient care or other related activities?
- What data are required by the application to support the intended use and workflow?
- Who will receive data/outputs from the use of the application?
- How will the overall patient/family experience be impacted by the use of the technology?

Once the processes impacted are determined, they are evaluated to identify the functions involved in the process. With this information, a multidisciplinary team can be created to study, document and discuss both the workflow and supporting technology. Benefits of this approach include:

- Enabling clinicians and others the rare opportunity to communicate with those outside their normal sphere of influence.
- Ensuring collaboration between IT and the clinical team.
- Documenting the process to help team members understand the bigger picture.
- Ranking the major issues of the process to provide a problem-solving hierarchy rather than the more typical daily "fire fighting."
- Creating a patient centered process rather than a provider focused process.

IPTA provides a guide for teams to systematically, yet efficiently achieve these goals. Figure 5-3 provides an overview of the IPTA steps and key activities in each step.

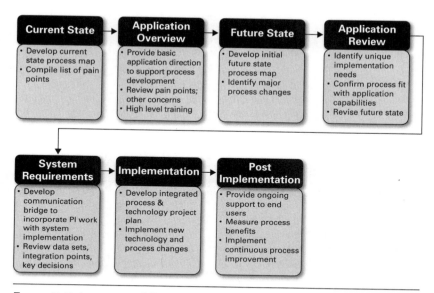

FIGURE 5-3: Integrated Process & Technology Approach.

Overall these actions will enable the staff to become more efficient in their daily processes, improve their quality of healthcare delivery and be proactive in the organization's approach to achieving Accountable Meaningful Use.

ITPA and Meaningful Use

Meaningful Use provides an excellent opportunity for hospitals and providers to make this transition into integrating clinical processes with IT. The Meaningful Use criteria can be aligned with impacted processes across the organization. A single process may impact the achievement of multiple criteria. By aligning the criteria to processes, organizations can determine where to focus their limited resources related to process integration efforts.

As a starting point, we have aligned the Stage 1 criteria with common patient processes in Figure 5-4. As reflected in the figure, processes impacted by new technology generally fall into one of four categories:

- Processes Associated with Direct Patient Care (e.g., Order Management, Medication Management).
- Processes to Support Care Delivery (e.g., Clinical Documentation, Registration and Assessment).
- Processes to Support Patient/Family Communication (e.g., Patient Education).
- Processes to Support Administrative Requirements (e.g., Health Management & Discharge, Reporting & Decision Support).

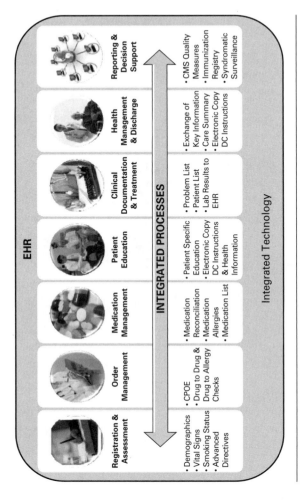

Figure 5-4: Meaningful Use Criteria and Process Alignment.

As an example, let us compare a traditional IT implementation approach to IPTA for a single Meaningful Use criteria—Record Smoking Status. In a traditional approach, organizations would answer the following "workflow" questions as a part of the implementation.

- Who will enter the data (e.g., registration, intake nurse)?
- Where will the data be entered (e.g., registration screen, admission assessment screen)?
- What report will be used for attestation? Core Measures? Quality Reporting?
- Who is responsible for running the report?
- Who is responsible for validating the accuracy of the report?

Often, these questions are answered by the implementation team and functional subject matter experts. In most organizations, many caregivers in multiple departments may ask the question "Do you smoke?" but, depending on the department and workflow, the answer may be recorded in one of many places in the EHR, potentially creating discrepancies in the way the information is mined and reported.

With IPTA, documenting the patient's smoking status is addressed as a part of the Registration and Admission Assessment processes. The cross-functional team begins by understanding how the information is used and its relationship to the patient information collection processes. By applying a Lean/Six Sigma philosophy, potential opportunities to reduce variation, eliminate duplication and streamline activities are identified. The focus is on understanding the flow of information from data collection to data utilization or extraction. The team should combine the information content with the system capabilities for recording and using information to create a best fit "future state" process. The application capabilities and patient flow process will determine the who, the when and the how that drives implementation and training decisions during deployment.

Recording smoking status provides an excellent example of how the criteria for future stages may influence the process. The Stage 1 criteria focus on organizations capturing the patient's smoking status. This information can be used to generate patient-specific lists or identify patient-specific education needs. Moving forward, integrating the smoking status of a patient into care planning and education plans will be essential to meeting anticipated requirements for developing longitudinal care plans for high-priority conditions, reporting patient status and other population management activities. In addition, other smoking statistics, such as second-hand smoke exposure will be integrated as part of the public health and population health management aspects of measurement.

It often helps to start with a "pilot" process to test, demonstrate and gain buy-in for the approach from key participants and senior leaders. Often, a less complicated process provides the right starting point. The organization is able to realize immediate benefits. Once in place, the principles of Lean, Six Sigma and other process improvement methods can be leveraged to evaluate the process. Using these proven tools, teams should:

- Identify the supporting processes and develop detailed workflow diagrams (Figure 5-5).
- Identify the IT mechanisms that support each of the minor processes and integrate flow of information into the workflow diagrams.

FIGURE 5-5: Process Redesign Framework.

- Identify the major issues with the process that lead to inefficiencies or poor quality.
- Identify what can be addressed in the short and long term through process and technology changes.
- Develop a project plan and leadership to implement the changes.
- Develop requirements to answer the Who, Where, What and How required for application implementation and training.

Develop Adoption Strategies

When asked to characterize physicians, many healthcare executives describe them as anarchic and incapable of working on a team or in a bureaucracy, overly reactive and self-serving. They are inclined to assert that physicians are poor planners, make rash decisions and do not share the same sense of loyalty to the institution as other stakeholders. The reality is that physicians are not a homogenous group but individuals with a spectrum of reactions to change, technology, evidence-based medicine, health reform etc. Physicians tend to exhibit healthy skepticism and to be critical of themselves and others, and their loyalty typically lies with their patients and physician colleagues with whom they have worked for years. In contrast, physicians' relationships with hospital leaders are typically far more tenuous. Mistrust and concern over control is often paramount because the skills that have allowed hospitals to run profitability and effectively have not always been successful in meeting the needs and managing the operations of physician practices.[94]

Historically, the relationship between the hospital and the physician has been a supplier-customer relationship. In recent years, hospitalists, intensivists and a variety of specialists including emergency medicine have become employees while primary care and certain specialties such as dermatology and endocrinology have moved further away from a relationship with the hospital. In fact, some physician groups have become competitors with investment in diagnostic, imaging and ambulatory surgical centers. Compounded by differences in age, gender and other factors, it is difficult to group physicians into a "one-size-fits-all" plan for IT adoption.

Adoption should be planned for just as one would plan for a system build or a move to a new facility. Important steps include:

- Understanding physician awareness and readiness.
- Segmenting physicians by level of readiness.
- Profiling physicians by leadership role.
- Developing a support structure for each physician readiness segment and leadership role.
- Organizing key activities, messages and results at key stages of adoption.

A survey of physicians can quickly segment physicians into one of four levels of adoption and readiness, as well as determine specific actions that should be taken to move them to the next level of adoption. Specific answers to questions such as:

- Have they implemented an EHR?
- What specific components of the EHR do they use?
- What are their greatest challenges with the practice-based EHR?
- Is the practice and/or hospital moving too fast, too slow or just right in regards to EHR implementation?
- If they could change one thing regarding technology deployment what would it be?
- What is their opinion regarding health information exchange?
- What type of support to they need to move to the next stage of EHR usage?
- Are they going to apply for the Meaningful Use incentives, and if so, when?

Once the survey is complete, physicians can be profiled by readiness segment and potential leadership role as shown in Figure 5-6.

To understand physician adoption, it is important to understand the traditional approach to physician education and learning. Over the

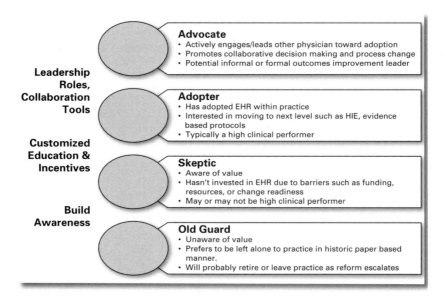

FIGURE 5-6: Profile of Physician Readiness and Leadership Role.

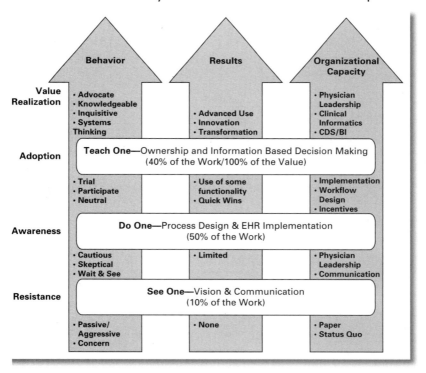

FIGURE 5-7: See-One, Do-One, Teach-One Adoption Model.

last decade, web-based tools, patient simulations and other educational approaches have flourished. While less acceptable and pervasive, the concept of "see one, do one and teach one" has a long track record in medical education. Physicians need hands-on learning experience. The opportunity to observe, trial, tinker and improve upon the tools will encourage their engagement and ultimately adoption.

One can assume that any clinician who has not adopted an EHR has some level of resistance. Whether passive or aggressive, the only way to change this is through specific messaging regarding the potential value addressing the WIIFM (*What's In It For Me*) concerns. At this stage, physicians only focus on the value of getting their own work done efficiently and profitability. At higher levels of adoption, physicians move to a "systems thinking" perspective, which considers the impact of their work on the effectiveness of the entire organization and healthcare delivery system.

Building upon the "see one, do one and teach one" approach,[95] as illustrated in Figure 5-7 and translating it to Meaningful Use adoption demonstrates the work, investment and infrastructure needed to support physicians as they progress through stages of Meaningful Use. Although returns and value are limited initially and investment is high, eventually, value is realized when transformation occurs.

Implement IT Systems

Implementation of EHRs is essential to achieving Meaningful Use but cannot be the only step in the process. The other key factors for success as outlined in this chapter (developing the decision-making structure and assigning accountability, designing processes and workflows and developing adoption strategies) must be addressed or the technology will not function as designed. Historically, when IT departments managed one major system implementation at a time, and the systems were not as mission critical as they are today, everything could be managed within IT. The complexity, interconnectedness and the dependencies among many of the Meaningful Use requirements means that efforts must be coordinated across users, across functional areas, across stakeholders and across care settings. The concept of the Project Management Office (PMO) was originally focused on providing IT implementation project management. In many organizations, the PMO has evolved into the eTMO (enterprise-Transformation Management Office) to manage large, complex organizational transformational initiatives, while retaining project management rigor and discipline.

TMOs typically report to a Chief Transformation Officer or other executive charged with organizational redesign. Best practice supports clear alignment of strategy, goals and work activities between the CIO and the clinical, medical staff and operational leadership.[96] With true clinical transformation, software and process change are reinforced with end-user adoption measures and application of change management principles. When people and management, technology and processes, leadership and vision all come together, clinical transformation is a powerful way to organize efforts to improve healthcare delivery.[97] Essential activities the eTMO oversees include:

- **Confirm that the technology being implemented is certified for Meaningful Use:** In addition to having the correct version of the vendor's technology, it must be implemented in the same fashion in which the vendor received certification. Code revisions or other adaptations that materially change the way the applications work will void the certification, and an organization will be unable to attest without self-certifying the technology.
- **Develop and implement effective communications plan:** As previously mentioned in the adoption planning section of this chapter, different stakeholders will require different messaging. The message should be tailored based on level of engagement, factors unique to the group such as function, familiarity with technology and specific requirements of the technology. The communications plan should specify objectives to be achieved, identification of stakeholder groups, the information each group needs to know, the medium through which messaging will occur and the message itself. Even in cases where the information communicated may be the same, the method by which it is delivered (newsletter, posting on bulletin board, email, intranet news, etc.), may vary depending on the audience. In addition, communication may vary based on the technology (and associated Meaningful Use objectives) being implemented. Finally, Meaningful Use communications should be aligned with enterprise strategy communications, such as value-based purchasing, clinical integration, quality improvement and other cross-venue care delivery initiatives.
- **Involve key stakeholders and end users in decisions:** End users should be involved in the planning and deployment of the technology, especially in areas that will affect workflow and usability of the system. In addition to the work of the IPTA, teams should consider screen configurations, drop-down lists construction and other factors that can be customized (while maintaining certification) during the

implementation. For clinical documentation that can be recorded in multiple areas of the EHR, gain consensus as to the one place an item will be documented. This will aid in mining, reporting and sharing clinical data.

- **Adjust training strategies to the audience:** The training needs and the most effective way to train users of the technology will vary depending on their role. Non-clinical functions such as registration or HIM may do well with a "train the trainer" approach and basic classroom training with an immediate "go-live." More complex clinical systems will require that super users be well-versed and available to clinicians as new functionality is rolled out. Many organizations provide one-on-one training and shadowing for physicians to make sure they are comfortable with the technology and so that any workflow issues can be addressed immediately.

- **Plan for continuous feedback:** Many organizations succeed in implementing the technology but fail to adjust and fine-tune the technology once it is in production. It is critical to monitor the effectiveness of workflows and address any functionality issues to ensure clinicians will use the system as intended. This will help reduce the amount of work-arounds that users often create to make the technology mirror their old workflows. Finally, working closely with clinicians on an ongoing basis will help maintain and improve adoption rates.

Table 5-2 details the differences between PMOs and TMOs.

TABLE 5-2: Comparison of PMO and TMO Capabilities.

PMO Capabilities (Basic)	TMO Capabilities (Advanced)
High Level Communication	Change Management
Integration with Operations	Negotiation
Business Case Development	Shared Vision
Project Planning	Standardization
Status Reporting	Patient Focused Approach
Project Tracking	Integrated Approach
Outcomes Measurement	Implementation Management
Integrated Performance Improvement	Enablement Management
Resource Management	Influence

(Continued)

TABLE 5-2: (Continued)

PMO Capabilities (Basic)	TMO Capabilities (Advanced)
Comprehensive Tool Kit	Project Life-Cycle Management
Training & Education	Evidence Based
Program Coordination	Portfolio Management
Leadership Alignment	Transparency
Strategic Alignment	Clinical Integration
Executive Championship	Collaborative Governance
Operations Driven	
Socialization	

Conclusion

Realizing value will require extensive work within the organization as described in this section. It will also necessitate coordinating with those who share and use information outside the walls of your organization to ensure that maximum value is realized not only for the enterprise but for the patient.

Chapter 6

Value Optimization

Susan Irby

> *"Measurement is the first step that leads to control and eventually to improvement.*
> *If you can't measure something, you can't understand it.*
> *If you can't understand it, you can't control it. If you can't control it, you can't improve it."*
>
> H. James Harrington

The Value Optimization phase of the Value Management Process is often overlooked in large-scale change projects. Failure to continuously monitor and report performance may not only result in failure to optimize the value of your investment but may mean that opportunities to realize additional value will be missed (see Figure 6-1).

This chapter focuses on Value Optimization and includes the following components:

- Measurement's role in the Value Management Framework.
- Adoption of tools and technologies.
- Development and execution of mitigation strategies and optimization plans.
- Expansion of the circle of influence.

Healthcare organizations are often "data rich" but "information poor." Expectations are set fairly high for the value that will result from the implementation of EHRs and other clinical systems. Often, organizations do not plan for the disruptions that will occur from deployment of IT and are never able to realize, much less optimize, the value of the systems.

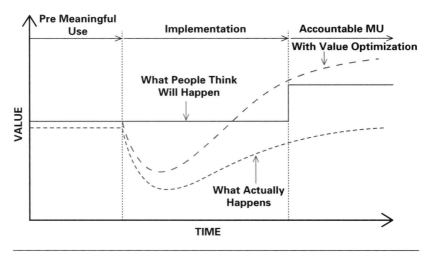

FIGURE 6-1: Value Optimization.

Measurement's Role in the Value Management Framework

Measuring value is more than calculating a financial return on investment. Instead it is identifying the things that matter to an organization, setting goals, measuring progress against those goals, communicating results and acting on those results for continuous improvement. While often used in conjunction with Lean or Six-Sigma techniques as part of performance improvement initiatives, the PDCA approach can be applied to the Value Management Framework. The Plan-Do-Check-Act (PDCA) cycle is illustrated in Figure 6-2.[98] The measurement steps associated with each phase of the Value Management Framework include:

- Value Definition—Identify Value Metrics.
- Value Realization—Collect Value Metrics.
- Value Optimization—Trend Value Metrics and Continuous Improvement.

As the organization plans for Accountable Meaningful Use, recognition of the relationship between financial and clinical measures for compliance reporting and value management is important. Identifying value metrics occurs simultaneously with the steps of understanding the Meaningful Use value lever, aligning with the transformation strategy and making stakeholders aware of the desired results. High-performing organizations will look comprehensively across all three stages of Meaningful Use to

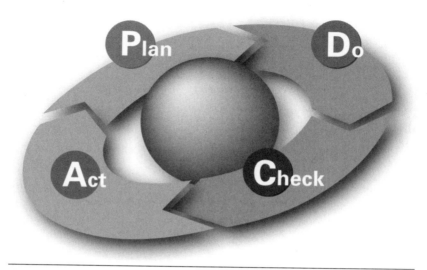

FIGURE 6-2: Plan-Do-Check-Act (PDCA) Cycle.

develop a measurement plan, not one stage at a time, in order to identify value metrics. Whether clinical, operational or financial in nature, a value measure will be:

- Derived from evidence.
- Focused on process and desired outcome.
- Precisely defined, with a standard means of calculation and a clear understanding of what is included and excluded from the measure, a clearly stated data source, identification of sampling (where appropriate) and set timeframes.
- Collectable and reliable.
- Understandable from a scoring and display perspective.
- Comparable to a stated goal or benchmark.
- Able to show progress over time.
- Actionable.

Value measures associated with Accountable Meaningful Use should not exist in a vacuum. Instead, organizations need to conduct an inventory of existing metrics, streamline and harmonize efforts across initiatives and integrate reporting. Incorporate measurement into process redesign, adoption planning and system implementations to prioritize investments for Accountable Meaningful Use. This will ensure EHRs and workflows are hardwired to incorporate measurement as part of the functionality.

Traditionally, hospitals and health systems have collected and stored transactional data that have been used to produce bills. With the advent of clinical systems and the EHR as part of Meaningful Use, a whole new world of data is now available for examination and use beyond the original intent of documenting care for reimbursement purposes (see Figure 6-3). Most healthcare providers have yet to capitalize on this precious asset, by analyzing and turning the data into actionable information.

According to a study reported by the MIT Sloan Management Review, top performing companies (across all industries) are three times more likely than lower performers to be sophisticated users of analytics.[99] High performing organizations typically have invested in the organizational capacity to use business intelligence and knowledge management skills and tools to improve performance.

HIMSS Analytics™ describes business intelligence as "A broad category of business processes, application software and other technologies for gathering, storing, analyzing and providing access to data to help users

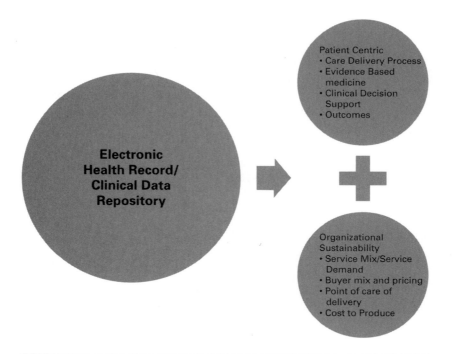

FIGURE 6-3: Enterprise Information Across the Care Continuum.

make better decisions. It can be described as the process of converting data into information and then into knowledge. Business intelligence provides sustainable competitive advantage, and is a valuable core competence."[100] Knowledge management is the actionable part of business intelligence that enhances an organization's ability and capacity to deal with and develop insights to support the dimensions of organizational mission, sustainability, performance and continuous improvement.[101] When score cards and reporting tools are integrated with new governance and decision-making structures, health system executives and clinical leaders will be armed with the necessary information to make critical decisions regarding service mix, cost management, outcomes improvement, care team composition and a variety of additional value producing initiatives.

Adopt and Adapt Tools and Technologies

Many tools and technologies collect raw data and transform them into useful management information. The EHR may serve as a data repository on its own or combined with multiple feeder systems that support data warehouses. Middleware designed to sit on top of the data repository can be used to generate the reports required for Meaningful Use (such as quality measures) and provide additional value measures including:

- Clinical effectiveness (outcomes).
- Clinical appropriateness (evidence and process).
- Patient and customer satisfaction.
- Safety (patient and staff).
- Access.
- Employee and medical staff satisfaction.
- Efficiency (cost).
- Financial.
- Privacy and security.
- Patient engagement.
- IT adoption.
- Timeliness.
- Population health.
- Public health.
- Community benefit.

One key factor for success in measuring value is the validity and completeness of the data used for reporting. It is essential that an audit procedure is in place to confirm that the information in the repository is consistent with the raw data that came from feeder systems or that would have been collected manually. In addition, the data must conform to expected values (e.g., expected range of values for height and weight). Decisions need to be made about missing data—if clinicians are not documenting the information in the EHR as structured data, it cannot be queried or mined to produce the metric. Changes in workflows may need to be made in order to ensure complete and correct data are documented in the EHR.

Value metrics should also collect cost information. A robust cost accounting approach should be used; the methodologies used for Medicare Cost Reports do not provide sufficient visibility into true costs to deliver care. Employing a cost-to-charge ratio [Total Expenses/Total Gross Charges times the Gross Charge for a single service (e.g., Head CT Scan)] does not reflect the true cost. Instead, organizations should examine direct costs in key cost categories (labor, supplies etc.), and the relative effort needed to deliver the care in order to determine costs at the procedure level.

As reimbursement structures evolve, it will be necessary to evaluate costs holistically across care settings in order to understand the total cost of care. This will require understanding not only hospital costs, but those in the primary care setting, specialists, long-term care, freestanding diagnostic centers (both lab and radiology), ambulatory surgery, home health and hospice, and public health delivery vehicles. Not a trivial effort, cross-venue costing will require collaboration across organizations to develop an understanding of the true cost of care for an episode (e.g., joint replacement), as well as for chronic conditions (e.g., congestive heart failure).

By linking quality and costs, organizations and communities can demonstrate the value of the care provided. Developing a reporting framework to communicate the value can take many forms. Scorecards that depict key indicators of performance are popular because they show results and progress graphically. Most business intelligence applications work with data repositories to produce executive level information, as well as granular scorecards. The ability to construct data "cubes" that deal with specific objectives and inquiries allows more in-depth analysis to determine sources of variance and other insights to help improve performance and deliver value.

Develop and Execute Mitigation Strategies and Optimization Plans

As progress towards all stages of Meaningful Use is being measured, gaps will be identified. It is not enough to identify the deficiencies—instead mitigation plans must be developed to address shortcomings in a timely manner in order to meet both internally-imposed goals and deadlines, as well as externally-mandated performance levels and completion dates.

The mitigation plan should identify the gap, as well as the type of risk or problem it poses. An example Clinical System Risk Taxonomy[102] is shown in Table 6-1. It breaks down project risk by dimension (is the problem people, process, technology etc.), as well as by specific factors that could be creating risk. By understanding what is impacting the ability to achieve the objective, a solution to address and reduce the risk can be identified.

TABLE 6-1: Clinical Systems Risks Taxonomies.

Risk Dimensions	Risk Factors
Technological	Introduction of a new technology
	Complex/unreliable technical infrastructure or network
	Complex software solution
	Complex/incompatible hardware
	Poor software performance
Human/User	Unrealistic expectations
	Overall resistance to change
	Lack of cooperation/commitment from users
	Poor computer skills
	Prior negative experiences with CIS projects
Usability	Poor perceived system ease of use
	Poor perceived usability system usefulness
	Misalignment of system with local practices and processes
Project team	Changes to membership on the project team
	Poor project leadership
	Lack of required knowledge or skills
	Lack of clear role definitions
	Negative attitude of project team members
Project	Large and complex project
	Project ambiguity

(Continued)

TABLE 6-1: (Continued)

Risk Dimensions	Risk Factors
	Changes to requirements
	Insufficient resources
	Lack of a project champion
	Lack of a formal project management methodology
Organizational	Lack of commitment from upper management
	Organizational instability
	Lack of local personnel knowledgeable in IT
	Environmental changes
Strategic/Political	Misalignment of actors' and partners' objectives and stakes
	Political games/conflict
	Unreliable external partners

It is also important to understand the relative impact of a particular risk. Impact is the combination of likelihood and consequences. In Table 6-2, these two factors are arrayed to describe the relative impact of not achieving an objective. Knowing both the type of risk, as well as the impact the risk can have will help frame the mitigation plan.

Listing the identified gaps, the types and impact of the risk of not addressing the gap, action step or steps to be taken, person or team to take the step, timeframe to accomplish (i.e., start and finish dates), any dependencies (e.g., cannot be completed until other steps are finished), resources required and the accountable executive; then provide the needed information for a Meaningful Use Mitigation Plan.

Planning for value optimization goes beyond just avoiding risks by setting new goals for performance. Once the mitigation plan is in place, the

TABLE 6-2: Risk Impact.

Likelihood	Consequences				
	Insignificant 1	Minor 2	Moderate 3	Major 4	Catastrophic 5
A- Almost Certain	High	High	Extreme	Extreme	Extreme
B- Likely	Moderate	High	High	Extreme	Extreme
C- Possible	Low	Moderate	High	Extreme	Extreme
D- Unlikely	Low	Low	Moderate	High	Extreme
E- Rare	Low	Low	Moderate	High	High

Value Management Framework can be applied to assess opportunities for value realization, and the appropriate value measures that can be tracked. Using the P-D-C-A (Plan-Do-Check-Act) philosophy described earlier, trends can be identified and performance taken to the next level for continuous value improvement.

Expand the Circle of Influence

High-performing organizations will make the right information available across the enterprise with the correct type of detail at each level based on the decisions being made. Departmental and service line scorecards may focus on day-to-day operations and measure progress toward improving the quality, safety and efficiency of care delivered. Senior leadership should be aware of more global goals including progress toward meeting all three stages of Meaningful Use.

Describing value delivered through Accountable Meaningful Use should expand beyond the organization to other key stakeholders. This should include any caregivers involved longitudinally across a care episode and/or those involved in the management of chronic conditions regardless of the setting. Business will want to see value delivered to their employees when care is provided. And payers will demand to see value in terms of improved quality and reduced costs.

Finally, in the new world of patient-centered care the healthcare consumer should be informed as to the value of the care they are receiving—whether it is a shorter length of stay in the hospital, reduction in unnecessary tests at the physician's office or avoiding a visit to the emergency department. Healthcare providers will need to translate these benefits, as well as the implications of clinical outcomes improvement efforts to patients, so they understand the resulting impact on their quality of life and wellness.

Chapter 7

High-Value Healthcare:
A Ten-Year Outlook

Pam Arlotto and Marla Crockett

"Imagine a future where a patient centered, community based care record drives the transformation of healthcare delivery: Clinicians become healthcare coordinators, working in partnership with patients to manage wellness; Patients undergo fewer tests and take fewer medications, reducing redundant and inappropriate care; Patients have a much better understanding of quality, cost, and outcomes; Hospitals compete based on the results they achieve rather than the grandeur of their buildings; Healthcare value improves, as quality, outcomes and cost reporting enables transparency; Patients have much more choice as consumers; Access to health information including genomes enables personalized medicine; treatments align with patient care preferences, risk taking thresholds, and physiology; and payers reimburse providers for quality rather than quantity."

(Adapted from) John D. Halamka, MD
Available online at: http://geekdoctor.blogspot.com/

Since the 1700s, U.S. hospitals have been the central point of communication and exchange of patient related information.[103] In the next decade, the patient-centered, interoperable EHR will replace the hospital as the primary vehicle for coordination of care. HITECH will have left its mark and, regardless of the timing and extent of the deployment of Stages 2 and 3, EHRs will have transformed the industry in significant ways including:

- The process of healthcare will be substantially digitized and electronically enabled. Managed care will switch from the role of restrictive gatekeeper to highly automated care management.
- Internet-informed patients will become partners with their healthcare providers in prevention and management of chronic disease.

- Health information exchanges will play significant roles in reinventing the roles of the Emergency Department, the primary care physician and other care providers.
- Patients will have access to providers 24-7 and at their convenience through virtual encounters.
- Medical decision making will be based on improved evidence, and "bench to bedside" time will be significantly reduced.
- Large quantities of hard data collected by EHR systems will be transferred to public health data repositories and be available for clinical research and improved bio-surveillance.

Progress for individual practitioners, hospitals and health systems will vary. Some will build on the requirements of HITECH to innovate and reengineer healthcare delivery practices. Others will hold onto the past and fail to make the transition. Success will depend on:

- Readiness and willingness to change.
- Capacity for accountability.
- Ability to collaborate to solve problems.
- Early investment in transformation and agility.

Transformation is the magic that happens when one evolves to the next level of understanding—when you are doing new things with technology that you could not have imagined doing when you started your journey. A great example of this is the typical person's experience pre- and post-Internet. Few of us could have imagined the impact it would have on our lives. Similarly, "winners" in high-value healthcare will take their use of EHRs to new levels, realize they have experienced a transformation and accomplish far more than they ever envisioned.[104]

Across the country, physicians and health systems are exploring new models of care delivery and examining the impact of fee reductions and the shift to value-based purchasing. Innovative models of care including Concierge Medicine, Virtual Clinics, Retail Clinics, Medical Tourism, eVisits, Complementary Medicine, Personalized Medicine, Clinical Institutes, etc. are challenging the status quo.

"New models" of care will focus on:

- New organizational structures forged among physicians, hospitals, medical groups, payers and patients.
- Comprehensive care management strategies and plans for patients with chronic conditions.

> "Create an innovative system of care and payment that result in measureable improved clinical outcomes and resource efficiency"
>
> "Focus on care requirements v. clinical diagnosis. This could be the most important decision healthcare leaders make. To get there, leaders will need to completely abandon traditional ways of organizing care"
>
> **ACOs, Bard & Nugent, 2011**

- A team approach to interdisciplinary, patient-centered care.
- Continuum-based care, throughout the life of the patient.
- Targeting high users of healthcare, especially older adults and the chronically ill.
- Elevating the role of nurses and transitioning from caregivers to "care integrators and/or coordinators."[105]
- Active engagement of the patient and her/his family in care planning and delivery.
- Reduction in variation in care through use of approved, best evidence-based treatment protocols/pathways.
- Leveraging technology, data and information for better decision making.
- Unwavering focus on satisfaction, quality and cost.

Two organizational forms are at the center of many strategies—the Patient Centered Medical Home (PCMH) and the Accountable Care Organization (ACO). Many agree that the two models build on and reinforce each other as a coherent, sustainable package of delivery system improvements. Additionally, they have the potential to provide more cost-effective disease prevention and management of patients with chronic illness.[106] When coupled with community and population health initiatives, the PCMH and ACO have the potential to create far-reaching population-based partnerships that emphasize disease prevention and health promotion.

The Patient Centered Medical Home (PCMH)

Demonstration projects at Group Health Cooperative of Puget Sound, Geisinger in Pennsylvania, and Intermountain Healthcare in Utah provide patients with a primary care physician and a team that can deliver personalized, whole person, coordinated care across conditions, episodes of care, providers and settings over time. The four key elements of the PCMH are:

- A commitment to primary care.
- An emphasis on the patient at the center of all activities.
- The implementation of "new model" practice.
- An association with increased payment incentives for the coordination of care.

"New Model" practice involves adoption of EHRs, implementation of the chronic care model including use of disease registries, guidelines, patient self-management support programs and continuous quality improvement initiatives.[107] Most practices today do not have the capacity or tools to transition to a PCMH. Value will have to be designed in through a combination of reengineering workflow, deployment of new EHR capabilities, linkage to health information exchanges and changing structural components of care delivery including point of care decision making, patient outreach and practice management. Transformation will involve establishing longer patient visit times, pairing physicians with extenders, establishing connectivity with patients, multidisciplinary care planning, use of "health maintenance reminders," cross continuum medication reconciliation, promotion of self-management workshops and new approaches to clinician compensation.[108]

Research indicates that the PCMH model is not a stand-alone delivery system innovation. It must be coupled with a larger entity that can bring in other components of the delivery system, provide resources, create economies of scale and implement accountability for performance; specifically, entities that accept responsibility for the cost and quality of care provided for a defined population of patients and provide the data on performance.[109]

Accountable Care Organizations

Accountable care will require a fundamental change in the perspectives of traditional healthcare organizations. New skills, tools and cultures will be necessary in order to:

- Improve the quality of care provided and the outcomes achieved.
- Optimize the utilization of services, with a focus on chronic disease management.
- Reduce the unit cost of care and eliminating waste, excess capacity and inefficiencies.

TABLE 7-1: Evolution of Care Models.

Care Today	Future Accountable Care
"We-They" Hospitals v. Physicians	Hospitals & Physicians on the Same Side
Cost Shifting	Bundled Payments
Success Based on Negotiation Prowess	Patient Centered
No Relationship Between Cost, Price, Quality, Value, Compensation	Data and Evidence Driven Care Decisions
Low Trust Across the Silos of Care	Focus on Chronic Disease Management and Prevention
Highly Variable Care	Innovative Solutions
Physician Accountable for Patient's Care	Coordinated Care Across Venues and Providers
Hospitals Accountable for Patients' Care	Measureable Quality and Outcomes
Competition	Demonstrated Value
EHR Implementation Focus	Health Information Exchange

The shift will be dramatic, as demonstrated in Table 7-1.

Delivering on Accountable Care

A number of leading entities have started to engage physicians, hospitals, payers and patients in the design and implementation of ACOs. In a recent survey of 13 ACOs, *Modern Healthcare* identified the following:

- Structures of ACOs are still evolving.
- Physicians are on-board in those surveyed, but hospitals and payers are lagging in participation.
- The majority of the ACOs are a separate legal entity.
- All are at break-even or profitable.
- The majority plan to seek Medicare certification.
- Leaders see the ACO as risky, but believe the risk of being left behind is greater.[110]

In addition to new organization models, new processes supported by EHRs, registries, health information exchange, and IT applications for population management, chronic disease management, cost management and member engagement will be needed. Specifics include those outlined in Table 7-2.

TABLE 7-2: New Processes/Systems Needed for Care Coordination and Accountable Care.[111]

Process	ACO Maturity		
	Early	Developing	Mature
ACO Member Engagement	Episode of care; Call center support;	Pre-care Intervention; Member outreach; Social media	Prevention; Lifestyle consultation; Remote monitoring; Social media
Cross Continuum Medical Management	Case management	Care Coordination; Patient centered; medical home	Disease management; Health maintenance
Clinical Information Exchange	Static; Read-only access; User request-based	Pushed (automatically) Continuity of care documents	Real time sharing across all venues; Patient access
Quality Reporting	EHR (Meaningful Use Stage 1)	EHR (Meaningful Use Stages 2 & 3)	Real time, dashboard/ desktop, ad hoc, reporting
Business Intelligence, Predictive Modeling And Analytics	Patient focused; Episode/encounter focused data; Retrospective; Clinical and financial	Population based; Continuum of care data; Predictive health analytics	Social and network data; Behavioral analytics; Real-time
ACO Risk And Revenue Management	Cost accounting across the continuum of care; Membership data management	Provider network management; Global contracting; Allocation of payment	Capitation management

To date, most of the success has been generated from targeted programs at existing integrated delivery systems such as Kaiser Permanente, Henry Ford Health System in Michigan, as well as some of the systems previously mentioned in the PCMH section. Additionally, large multi-specialty group practices such as the Cleveland Clinic in Ohio; Mayo Clinic in Minnesota, Florida and Arizona; Virginia Mason Clinic in Washington State; and Marshfield Clinic in Wisconsin have established results in specific demonstration projects. Physician Hospital Organizations such as Advocate Health System in Chicago, Independent Practice Associations such as the Hill Physician Group in California and virtual physician organizations such as Community Care of North Carolina provide opportunity in rural areas.

CMS has tested the ACO model under the Physician Group Practice Demonstration Project (PGP). Ten of the nation's most integrated groups had the "opportunity to earn performance payments derived from savings for improving quality and efficiency of healthcare delivery services through better coordination of care and investment in care." Among the brutal facts of this demonstration project, "the economic and market rewards (for ACOs) may not materialize for a long time .... none of the organizations (in the PGP) indicated a positive ROI related to improvement activities."[112]

Conclusion

Achieving high value for patients must become the overarching goal of the healthcare delivery system. While the appropriate care delivery and reimbursement models will be sorted out over the next few years, healthcare providers cannot wait until everything is sorted out to make necessary changes. The path toward accountability is clear; improve outcomes, reduce cost and transform today's fragmented health system into a coordinated, patient-focused "system of care" that is based on interoperable EHRs.

Today's information systems and organizational capacity make it difficult to measure and improve value. The Value Management Framework we have presented provides a sequence of activities including Value Definition, Value Realization and Value Optimization to help clinicians and other professionals focus on what matters most. Value Maps can provide tools for aligning with key strategies, understanding the Meaningful Use value lever, identifying the desired benefits and building stakeholder awareness. "As-Is" assessments coupled with understanding of best practices, inform the desired "Future State." Critical to realization of value is the appropriate decision-making structure, integrated process and technology design and enterprise Transformation Management.

Measurement is increasingly necessary to comply with external demands from CMS, The Joint Commission and a variety of other external agencies and groups. Healthcare payers and consumers are requiring providers to demonstrate their ability to provide high-quality care at fair prices while satisfying their customers. In order to realize value from investments in technology, Meaningful Use and transformation, healthcare providers need to develop a system of measurement that tracks a variety of quality and performance outcome measures. Baseline data and post interventional measurement analysis will highlight opportunities for continuous improvement. While the future is uncertain, ongoing measurement and attention to trends will inform decision making as organizations design new models of care and respond to reimbursement changes in the years ahead.

W. Edwards Deming in *Out of Crisis* said, "Innovation, the foundation of the future, cannot thrive unless top management has declared unshakeable commitment to quality ... the most important figures that one needs for management are unknown or unknowable but successful management must never the less take account of them."[113] To innovate and transform, the healthcare industry must make an unshakeable commitment to quality. Measuring, reporting and comparing outcomes will be the most important steps the healthcare industry can take toward rapidly improving outcomes and making good choices about reducing costs.[114]

References

1. Arlotto PW, Birch PC, Crockett MH, Irby SP. *Beyond Return on Investment: Expanding the Value of Health Information Technology.* Chicago: Healthcare Information & Management Systems Society, 2007.

2. Blumenthal D. Launching HITECH. *New England Journal of Medicine.* 2010;362:382–385.

3. Deloitte Center for Health Solutions, *Value-based Purchasing: A Strategic Overview for Healthcare Industry Stakeholders,* 2011.

4. Shortell SM. *Remaking Health Care in America: Building Organized Delivery Systems,* First Edition. Jossey-Bass Publishers, 1996.

5. Belmont E, Haltom CC, Hastings DA, et al. A New Quality Compass: Hospital Board's Increased Role Under the Affordable Care Act. *Health Aff.* 2011;30:7:1282.

6. IOM, *Crossing the Quality Chasm,* 2001.

7. Stewart M. Towards a global definition of patient centered care. *BMJ,* 2001.

8. Deloitte. Value-based Purchasing: A Strategic Overview for Health Care Industry Stakeholders. Available at www.deloitte.com/view/en_US/us/Insights/centers/center-for-health-solutions/82e4b2d e53ebe210VgnVCM1000001a56f00aRCRD.htm. Last accessed January 2012.

9. Glaser J. HITECH Lays the foundation for more ambitious outcomes-based reimbursement. *Am J Managed Care,* 2010; 16(12 Spec No.): SP19–SP23.

10. Markle Foundation. *Connecting for Care, Achieving the Health IT Objectives of the American Recovery and Reinvestment Act, A Framework for 'Meaningful Use' and 'Certified or Qualified' EHR;* 2009.

11. Arlotto PW, Oakes J. *Return on Investment: Maximizing the Value of HIT* Chicago: Healthcare Information & Management Systems Society, 2003.

12. Deloitte. Value-based Purchasing: A Strategic Overview for Health Care Industry Stakeholders. Available at www.deloitte.com/view/ en_US/us/Insights/centers/center-for-health-solutions/82e4b2d e53ebe210VgnVCM1000001a56f00aRCRD.htm. Last accessed January 2012.

13. Bard M, Nugent M. *Accountable Care Organizations: Your Guide to Strategy, Design and Implementation.* Chicago: Health Administration Press, 2011.

14. PriceWaterhouseCoopers. Ready or not: On the road to meaning-ful use of EHRs and health IT, A Thought Leadership Piece, 2010.

15. Arlotto PW. *Journey to High Value Healthcare: the Board's Role in Clinical Transformation*, Center for Healthcare Governance, 2011.

16. Kenney C., *Transforming Health Care: Virginia Mason Medical Center's Pursuit of the Perfect Patient Experience.* New York: CRC Press, 2010.

17. Markle et al, *Collaborative Comments on the Centers for Medicare and Medicaid Services' Notice of Proposed Rule Making for the Electronic Health Record Incentive Program* (CMS-033-P), March 15, 2010.

18. Adapted from Warren McFarlan. *IT Changes the Way You Compete. Harvard Business Review.* May–June 1998, 98–103.

19. Arlotto PW. *Journey to High Value Healthcare: The Board's Role in Clinical Transformation*, AHA Center for Healthcare Monograph, 2011.

20. Sinno M, Gandhi S, Gamble M. 8 Problems surrounding mean-ingful use. *Beckers Hospital Review*, April 28, 2011.

21. Accenture. *Finding Meaning in Meaningful Use Insights into Achieving EMR Success*, 2010.

22. McKinsey. Reforming hospitals with IT investment. *McKinsey on Business Technology.* 2010;20.

23. Accenture. *Secrets of Success on the EMR Journey to Meaningful Use: Leading Hospital CIOs Reveal Key Lessons Learned.* January 2010.

24. Multiple Sources.

25. HIMSS LinkedIn Group.

26. Arlotto PW, Oakes J. Return on Investment: Maximizing the Value of Healthcare Information Technology, Chicago: HIMSS, 2003.

27. Dorgran SJ, Dowdy JJ. When IT Lifts Productivity. London School of Economics- McKinsey survey, McKinsey-Research Brief, 2004.

28. ASUG/SAP. *Value Realization: Achieving Business Value from Your IT Investments.* 2007.

29. Collins English Dictionary—Complete & Unabridged. 10th Ed, 2009.

30. Weed LL. Medical records that guide and teach. *New Engl J Med.* 1968;278:593–599.

31. Best Practice Considerations for Problem Lists. Available online at: www.AHIMA.org. Last accessed December 2011.

32. Jones SS, Heaton P, Friedberg MW, Schneider EC. *Health Aff.* 2011 30:2005–2012; published ahead of print September 14, 2011, doi:10.1377/hlthaff.2011.0245.

33. Adapted from Hunter and Westerman, The Real Business of IT: How CIOs Create and Communicate Value. *Harvard Business Press*, 2009.

34. Available online at: http://management-quotes.net/author/Russell_Ackoff. Last accessed December 2011.

35. Kaplan R, Porter M. Three Myths About Health Care Exploded. *Harvard Business Review*, September 2011.

36. Congressional Budget Office. *Technological change and the growth of health care spending*, Washington DC: CBO: January 2008.

37. Finklestein E. Annual Medical Spending Attributable to Obesity: Payer and Service Specific Estimates. *Health Aff.* 2009;28(5).

38. Roehrig C. Rousseau D. The Growth in Cost Per Case Explains
     Far More of US Health Spending Increases Than Rising Disease
     Prevalence. *Health Aff.* September 2011.

39. Kohn LT., Corrigan JM, Donaldson MS. To Err Is Human:
     Building a Safer Health System. Committee on Quality of Health
     Care in America—Institute of Medicine, National Academies
     Press, Washington, D.C.

40. 42 CFR Parts 412, 413, 422 et al., Medicare and Medicaid
     Programs; Electronic Health Record Incentive Program; Final
     Rule, July 28, 2010.

41. 2010 AHA Environmental Scan: *It is likely that all hospital boards
     will have a committee or subcommittee on hospital quality and patient
     safety by 2014.*

42. Healthcare Information and Management Systems Society on
     the Internet. Available online at: www.himss.org. Last accessed
     December 2011.

43. Department of Health and Human Services, Centers for Medi-
     care and Medicaid Services, Final Rule, Federal Register/
     Vol. 75, No. 144/Wednesday, July 28, 2010/Rules and Regula-
     tions, Page 44332. Available online at: http://www.scribd.com/
     doc/35039865/Electronic-Health-Record-Incentive-Program-
     Final-Rule-2010-17207. Last accessed December 2011.

44. Forrest CB, Glade GB, Baker AE, Bocian A, vonSchrader S,
     Starfield B. Coordination of specialty referrals and physician sat-
     isfaction with referral care. *Arch Pediatric Adolescent Medicine.*
     2000;154:499–506.

45. Bodenheimer T. Coordinating Care-a perilous journey through the
     health care system. *New Engl J Med.* 2008 358(10):1064–1071.

46. Transitions of Care Measures. A Paper by the NTOCC Measures
     Work Group, 2008.

47. National Transitions of Care Coalition, Improving transitions of
     care; findings and considerations of the 'vision of the National
     Transitions of Care Coalition. September 2010.

48. Institute of Medicine. *Preventing Medication Errors*. Washington, DC: National Academies Press; 2006.

49. Rozich JD, Howard RJ, Justeson JM, et al. Patient safety standardization as a mechanism to improve safety in health care. Jt. Comm J Qual Saf. 2004;30(1):5–14.

50. Cornish PL, Knowles SR, Marchesano R, et al. Unintended medication discrepancies at the time of hospital admission. *Arch Intern Med*. 2005;165:424–429.

51. *Joint Commission Perspectives*®. Joint Commission on Accreditation of Healthcare Organizations. Volume 31, Issue 1 Copyright 2011, January 2011.

52. Federal Register, Department of Health and Human Services. Centers for Medicare & Medicaid Services, 42 CFR Parts 412, 413, 422 et al. Medicare and Medicaid Programs; Electronic Health Record Incentive Program; Final Rule, July 28, 2010;44362.

53. United States Pharmacopeia. Medication errors involving reconciliation failures. In: *Patient Safety CAPSLink* [online]. 2005 Oct [cited 2006 Jan 10].

54. Agency for Healthcare Quality Research. Patient Safety Primers, Medication Reconciliation. Available online at: www.AHRQ. gov; Publication available at: http://psnet.ahrq.gov/primer. aspx?primerID=1. Last accessed December 2011.

55. Aspden P, Wolcott J, Bootman JL, Cronenwett LR, Eds. *Preventing Medication Errors: Quality Chasm Series Committee on Identifying and Preventing Medication Errors*. National Academies Press, 2006.

56. Federal Register, Department of Health and Human Services Centers for Medicare & Medicaid Services, 42 CFR Parts 412, 413, 422 et al. Medicare and Medicaid Programs; Electronic Health Record Incentive Program; Final Rule, July 28, 2010;44362.

57. Poon EG, Blumefeld B, Hamann C, et al. Design and implementation of an application and associated services to support interdisciplinary medication reconciliation efforts at an integrated healthcare delivery network. *J Am Med Inform Assoc*. 2006;13:581–592.

58.   Chronic Care: A Call to Action for Health Reform. Washington: AARP Public Policy Institute, 2009.

59.   Hibbard JH, Mahoney ER, Stock R, Tusler M.Do Increases in Patient Activation Result in Improved Self-Management Behaviors?" *Health Services Research.* 2007.

60.   Case Study: Giving Patients More Control. *HFMA: Leadership, 2011.*

61.   Chronic Care: A Call to Action for Health Reform. Washington: AARP Public Policy Institute, 2009.

62.   Eagan MC. Bariatric Surgery: Malpractice Risks and Risk Management Guidelines. *The American Surgeon.* 2005:369–375.

63.   United States, Department of Health & Human Services, *Medicare and Medicaid Programs; Electronic Health Record Incentive Program; Proposed Rule.* Washington: Centers for Medicare & Medicaid Services, 2010. 1851.

64.   National Priorities and Goals: Aligning Our Efforts to Transform America's Healthcare. Washington: National Quality Forum; 2008.

65.   Robert Wood Johnson Foundation. Care About Your Care. Webcast launch on Sept 15, 2011. Available on the Care About Your Care Channel on YouTube at: www.youtube.com/watch?v=QpnqJEgISq4. Last accessed January 2012.

66.   Bush GW. State of the Union Address 2004. Available online at: http://stateoftheunionaddress.org/2004-george-w-bush#ixzz1CdKe6Mui. Last accessed December 2011.

67.   Available online at: http://healthit.hhs.gov/portal/server.pt/community/healthit_hhs_gov__onc/1200. Last accessed December 2011.

68.   Available online at: http://www.hhs.gov/healthit/valueHIT.html Last accessed December 2011.

69.   Available online at: http://healthit.hhs.gov/portal/server.pt?open=512&objID=1487&parentname=CommunityPage&parentid=28&mode=2&in_hi_userid=11113&cached=true. Last accessed December 2011.

70. Available online at: http://healthcare-economist.com/2010/01/26/ what-are-accountable-care-organizations/. Last accessed December 2011.

71. Conway P, Goodrich K, Machlin S, Sasse B, Cohen J. Patient-centered care categorization of U.S. health care expenditures. *HSR: Health Services Research* April 2011;46(2),479–490.

72. Congressional Budget Office. *High-cost Medicare Beneficiaries.* A CBO Paper. May 2005. Available online at: www.cbo.gov/showdoc. cfm?index=6332&sequence=0. Last accessed December 2011.

73. Walunas T. Finding a Personal Meaning in Meaningful Use. March 16, 2011. Available online at: www.healthit.gov/buzz-blog/ ehr-case-studies/finding-personal-meaning-meaningful/. Last accessed December 2011.

74. Wright A, Sittig DF, Ash JS, et al. Development and evaluation of a comprehensive clinical decision support taxonomy: comparison of front-end tools in commercial and internally developed electronic health record systems. *J Am Med Informatics Assoc.* 2011;18:232e242. doi:10.1136/amiajnl-2011-000113.

75. Encyclopedia of Public Health. Available online at: www. enotes.com/public-health-encyclopedia/history-public-health. Last accessed December 2011.

76. Available online at: www.healthypeople.gov/2020/about/default. aspx. Last accessed December 2011.

77. Available online at: http://www.healthypeople.gov/2020/about/ QoLWBabout.aspx. Last accessed December 2011.

78. Available online at: http://www.naphit.org/default.asp. Last accessed December 2011.

79. Crofton J. (2004). The MRC randomized trial of streptomycin and its legacy: a view from the clinical front line. *JLL Bulletin:* Commentaries on the history of treatment evaluation. Available at www.jameslindlibrary.org.

80. Kahn MD. *Integrating Electronic Health Records and Clinical Trials, An Examination of Pragmatic Issues.* University of Colorado, The Children's Hospital, 2006.

81. Available online at: www.clinicaltrials.gov, 2008. U.S. National Library of Medicine. Last accessed October 2011.

82. Miller MD. The EHR Solution to Clinical Trial Recruitment in Physician Groups. *Health Management Technology*, August 2009.

83. Third Annual HIMSS Security Survey Final Report. Health Information Management Systems Society, 2010.

84. Blumenthal, D. Building Trust in Health Information Exchange. Statement on Privacy and Security. Available on the ONC website at http://healthit.hhs.gov/portal/server.pt?CommunityID=2994& spaceID=11&parentname=CommunityEditor&control=SetCom munity&parentid=9&in_hi_userid=11673&PageID=0&space= CommunityPage. Last accessed January 2012.

85. Institute for Health Technology Transformation, 2010, Top Ten Things You Need to Know About Engaging Patients. United States, Office of the National Coordinator for Health Information Technology *Building Trust in Health Information Exchange: Statement on Privacy and Security* (Washington, U.S. Department of Health and Human Services, 2010).

86. Bernd DL, Fine PS. Electronic Medical Records: A Path Forward. *Frontiers of Health Services Management*, Fall 2011.

87. Hovet C. *Governance & Leadership—The Support Structure for "Meaningful Use of your Electronic Health Record (EHR)*, MEDITECH Solutions Group within Dell Services.

88. Belmont E, Haltom CC, Hastings DA, et al. A New Quality Compass: Hospital Boards' Increased Role Under The Affordable Care Act. 10.1377/hlthaff.2010.1317. *Health Aff.* 30, 7 (2011): 1282–1289.

89. Mountford J, Webb C. When Clinicians Lead. *McKinsey Quarterly*, February 2009.

90. Adapted from Meaningful use: Instituting effective infrastructure and implementation governance. Deloitte Development LLC 2011.

91. The Cornerstones of Accountable Care. Valence Health. 2010.

92. Ibid.

93. Thomas HL. Turning Doctors into Leaders. *Harvard Business Review*. April 2010:53.

94. Lister E, Sagin T. Creating the Hospital Group Practice. ACHE Management Series, Chicago; 2009.

95. Adapted from Tom Fee. *Adoption Planning Tiers*. Available online at: www.veritypartnersllc.com. Last accessed December 2011.

96. Staley-Sirois ML, Konschak CB. Organizational Structures for Clinical Transformation. Divurgent. Available at: http://divurgent.com/images/ClinicalTransformation.pdf. Last accessed January 2012.

97. Evans, CC. Rethinking 'Clinical Transformation'. *Healthcare IT News*, August 2009.

98. Bulsuk, KG. Available online at: www.bulsuk.com. Last accessed December 2011.

99. LaValle S, Hopkins MS, Lesser E, Shockley R, Kruschwitz N. Analytics: The New Path to Value. MIT Sloan Management Review Research Report, MIT Sloan Management Review and the IBM Institute for Business Value, Fall 2010.

100. HIMSS Analytics™ Database, 2001.

101. Bellinger G. Knowledge Management. 1997. Available online at www.systems-thinking.org/tkco/tkco.htm. Last accessed December 2011.

102. Paré G, Sicotte C, Jaana M, Girouard D. Prioritizing Clinical Information System Project Risk Factors: A Delphi Study. Proceedings of the 41st Hawaii International Conference on System Sciences; 2008.

103. Seymour D. *Hospitals 2020 How Fundamental Economics, Clinical Innovation, and IT will Reshape the Healthcare Delivery Model*. Presentation to SHSMD, September 2009.

104. Allscripts. *The Electronic Physician*, Allscripts Healthcare Solutions, 2005.

105. Joynt J, Kimball B. *Innovative Care Delivery Models: Identifying New Models that Effectively Leverage Nurses.* Presented to Robert Wood Johnson Foundation, January, 2008.

106. Shortell G. Wu. United States Innovations in Healthcare Delivery. *Public Health Reviews*, Vol. 32, Number 1.

107. Ibid.

108. Ibid.

109. Ibid.

110. Forging the Way: ACOs taking hold despite loose definitions, with different methods—and varying results. *Modern Healthcare.* 2011;18:6–7, 18, 20, 22, 24.

111. Enders T, Battani J, Zywiak W. Health Information Requirements for Accountable Care. Computer Science Corporation. 2010; p1–12.

112. Kaufman NF. Three brutal facts that provide strategic direction for healthcare delivery systems. *Journal of Healthcare Management.* May/June 2011.

113. Deming WE. *Out of Crisis*, Massachusetts Institute of Technology. 1986.

114. Porter, ME. What is Value in Healthcare. *New Engl J Med.* December 2010.

Index

A

Accountability for system performance, 9
Accountable Care Organization (ACO), 145, 146–149
Accountable Meaningful Use of EHRs, 11, 17. *See also* Value realization processes
Admission, discharge, transfer (ADT) interface, 18
Admission/intake process, 66–67, 74
Affordable Care Act (ACA), 5
American Recovery and Reinvestment Act (ARRA) of 2009, 2, 13
American Society for Testing and Materials (ASTM), 27
At-risk populations, preventive care for, 42–43

B

Back-office projects, 16
Berwick, Donald, 11
Beyond Return on Investment: Expanding the Value of Healthcare Information Technology, 1–2
Board of Directors/Board of Trustees, 112

C

Care planning, 88, 95
Case management and discharge, 52–53, 60, 74, 89, 95
Centers for Medicare & Medicaid Services (CMS), 5
Chief Clinical Quality Officer (CCQO), 45
Chief Executive Officer (CEO), 45
Chief Medical Information Officer (CMIO), 50, 59
Chief Medical Officer (CMO), 59, 66
Chief Nursing Officer (CNO), 66
Chief Operating Officer (COO), 45
Chief Transformation Officer, 130
Clinical decision support systems, 45–46, 101
Clinical documentation, 39–40, 45, 60, 82, 88–89
Clinical Institutes, 144
Clinical integration, 6, 118

W